Somewhere Between

WAR and PEACE

KEHRER

by James Hill

Through a Different Lens

Whenever I look at one of my photographs, some version of the scene plays out again in my mind's eye. It isn't long, usually just a few seconds—a brief cinematic recollection filled with sound and movement, a return to moments buried deep within my memory. Their vividness often unsettles me, as do the thoughts they evoke. Even though these instants may be frozen visually, many remain for me emotionally unresolved, still demanding my attention years after I first witnessed them.

I have learned that I cannot escape these images, no matter how rarely or how often I might look at them. Filled with fears and fondness, they represent the collected memories of hundreds of journeys, decades of work. When considered together, they force me to confront not only their own ambiguities but also the conundrum faced by any photographer attempting to piece together the kaleidoscope of a past, one image at a time.

When I set out on this photographic life, I was eager to see to anything and everything. I wanted to capture the world's joys and follies, indifferent as to whether I portrayed hope or sorrow, embracing both with equal curiosity. Yet, over time, a darkness began to encroach. The moments of violence hardened me without my realising, returning me a stranger to those I loved. I could still marvel at the infinite whiteness of the Arctic or the golden warmth of an Italian afternoon, but in my dreams, again and again, I would find myself being pulled to an edge beyond which there was nothing. I would fall and fall before waking in my bed or sleeping bag, soaked in sweat and startled to be alive.

It takes a far finer balance than I ever imagined to live with the past, just as it does to stand, physically and emotionally, in a scene, knowing what to watch and when to move. These images, circulating like old slides on a Kodak carousel, have become ingrained in my consciousness; the more powerful the image, the deeper its hold. I am caught between the duty to remember and the desire to erase.

My photographs remind me not only where I've been but also what it has taken for me to get home again. For each journey between the familiar and those places where life and death are weighed on another set of scales is a voyage through an emotional no-man's-land, somewhere between war and peace.

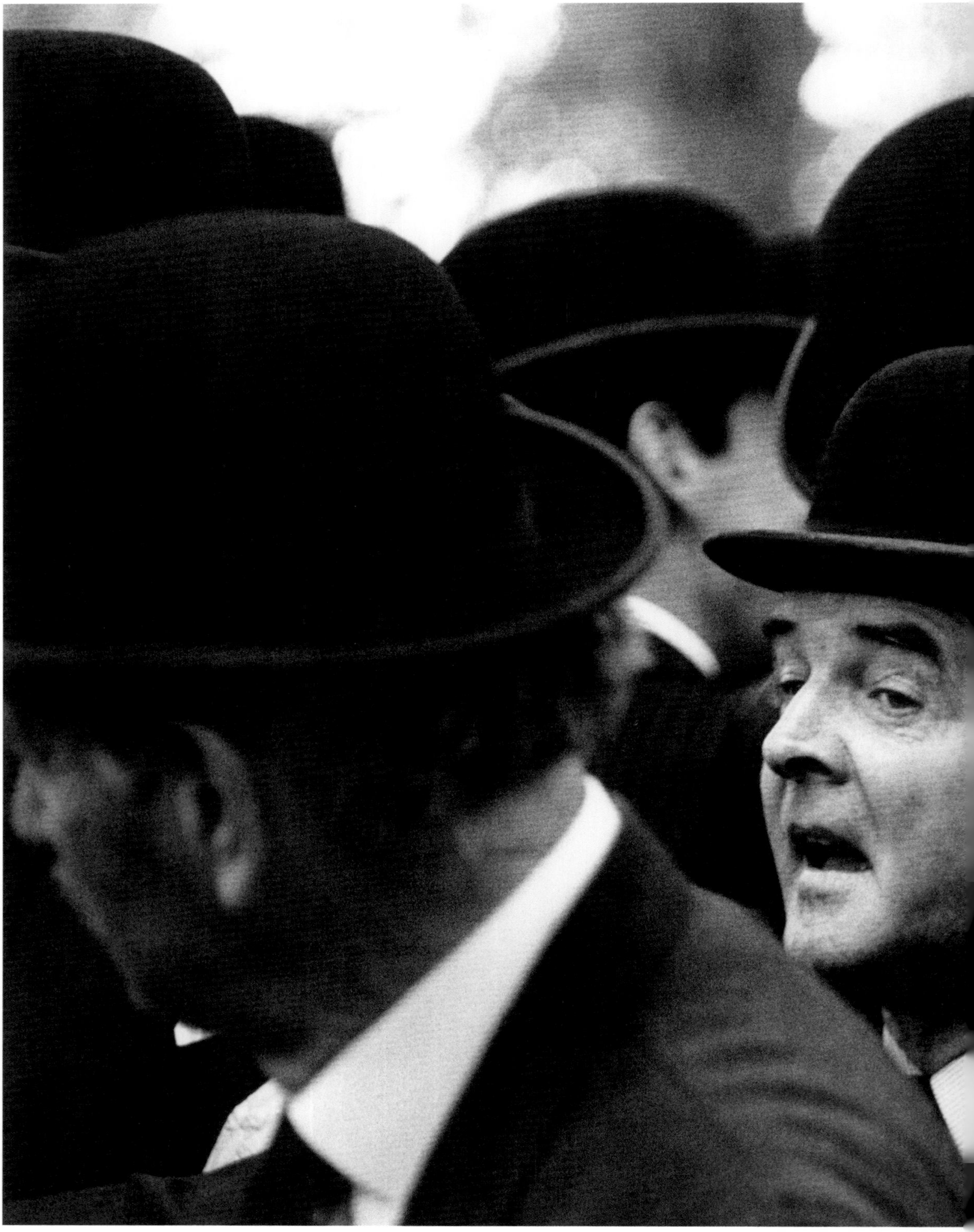

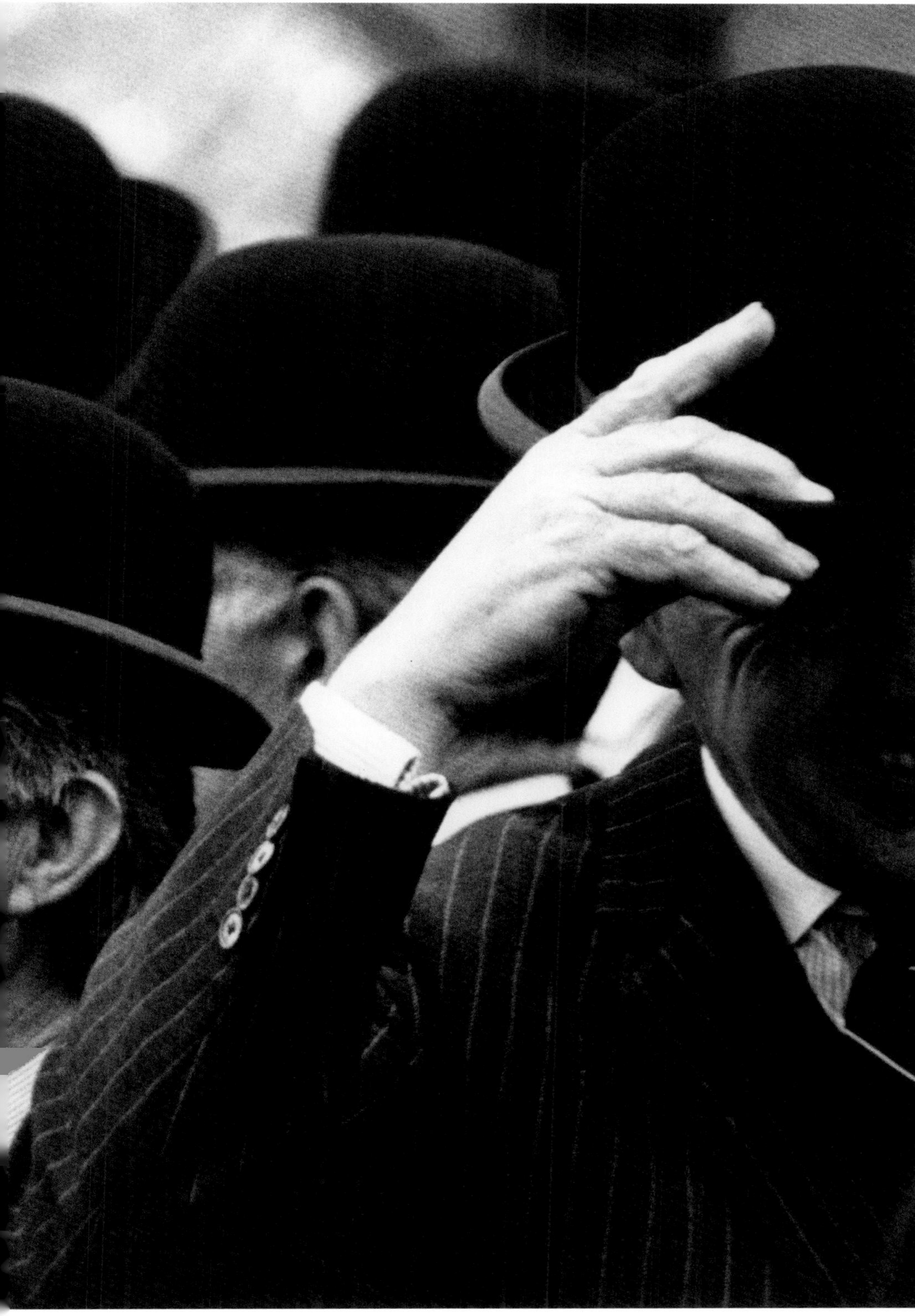

As a young man, my father served in the Parachute Regiment of the British Army and became an officer, joining the Army Reserve only after being wounded during an operational jump in 1952. When the Suez crisis broke, in 1956, he was nevertheless called up; he was told to report to Goodge Street Tube Station, in central London, wearing a dark suit and a bowler hat, and carrying an umbrella. The hat and the umbrella were presumably to camouflage the fact that he was being ordered to invade a country in the Middle East. Luckily for him, my parents later explained to me, he missed both the rendezvous and the Suez conflict because he was in bed with glandular fever. In fact, I never saw him wear a bowler hat—even though he kept one in the cupboard above his coats, just in case.

Many years later, when I left university in the summer of 1988, I was offered the chance to join my father in the City of London with a position in corporate finance at Lazard Frères. But I had no desire to follow in his footsteps; after three years studying history at Oxford, I yearned to explore the world, not the London Underground. So I took a year off to travel in Australia and Asia, assuring my parents that I would accept the position on my return. Instead, still lacking any desire to pursue a career in business, I began tutoring at a private college in London to make ends meet, all the while longing to resume my travels.

During my year off, I used an SLR camera for the first time—a Pentax P30 with a wide-angle lens and a long

Answering the Call

London
May 1991

zoom—and I fell in love with that camera. Encountering the world through its viewfinder was extraordinarily liberating. As I pondered my future during those tutorials on Tudor politics, I impulsively decided that instead I wanted to capture history as it was being made, and that photography would be my life. Soon afterwards, I announced to a close friend from university that I was going to become a photojournalist. He paused before replying. "And next week," he inquired, "you're going to be an astronaut?"

Of course, I didn't have a clue as to how to pursue my objective, but I started by devouring the monographs of famous photographers. Seduced by the exotic cocktail of romance and danger offered by the example of Robert Capa and the other Magnum founders, I applied for a place on the postgraduate course in photojournalism at the London College of Printing in 1990. Despite having a portfolio composed solely of photographs that I had taken in Asia during my travels, I was accepted. The college was in Elephant and Castle, in south London. I immediately went out and bought some black clothes.

Each week the students had to produce a story with pictures and a text. There were twenty-four of us on the course—dreamers mostly, who had barely considered the mundane challenges of supporting oneself with one's camera, let alone the physical risks involved if anyone was unwise enough to hire us. And Trevor Jones, our course director, was in his own fog of romanticism, arriving each day at school in a tweed jacket, corduroys, and a knitted tie. Although this was only ten years before the digital revolution in photography, he was still grappling with the complexities of 35mm film, waxing nostalgically about the days when press photographers worked with double dark slides and large-format cameras.

That year was, mercifully, a process of learning, of pretending to be a photojournalist without facing the realities of what it actually entailed. The dangers that lay ahead of us were almost impossible to imagine. Paul Jenks, with whom I had also been at boarding school, would be killed only two years later: shot near Osijek, in Croatia, in January 1992, he bled to death before help could arrive. And James Miller, who went on to become an award-winning documentary filmmaker, would be killed by Israeli forces in Gaza, in May 2003.

Of all the pictures that I took that year, it is only this one—of retired cavalry officers chatting before their annual parade in Hyde Park—that I now regard with any pride or pleasure. It reminds me of my father on the walk that never was, in his dark suit and bowler hat, carrying a long black umbrella, decades before I myself went off to war.

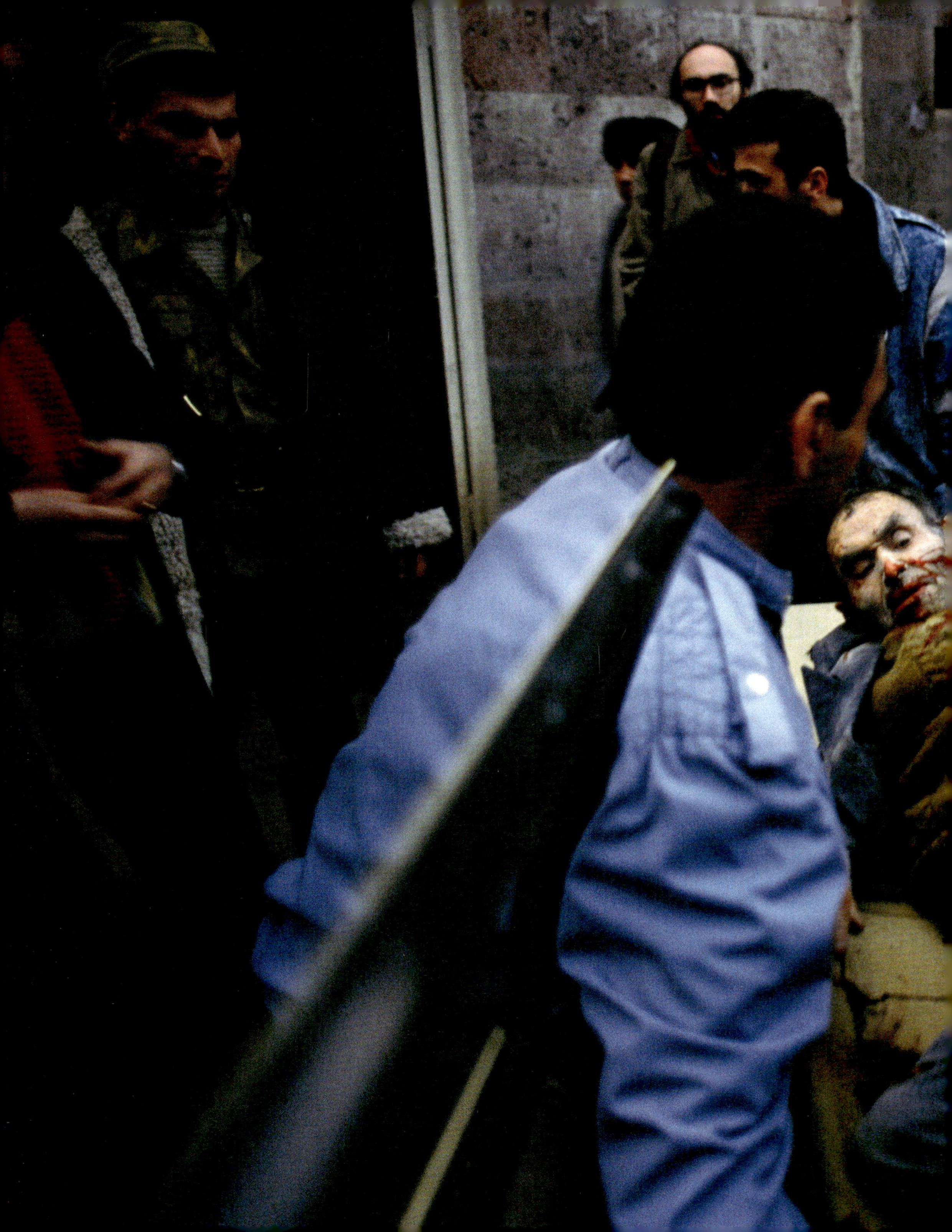

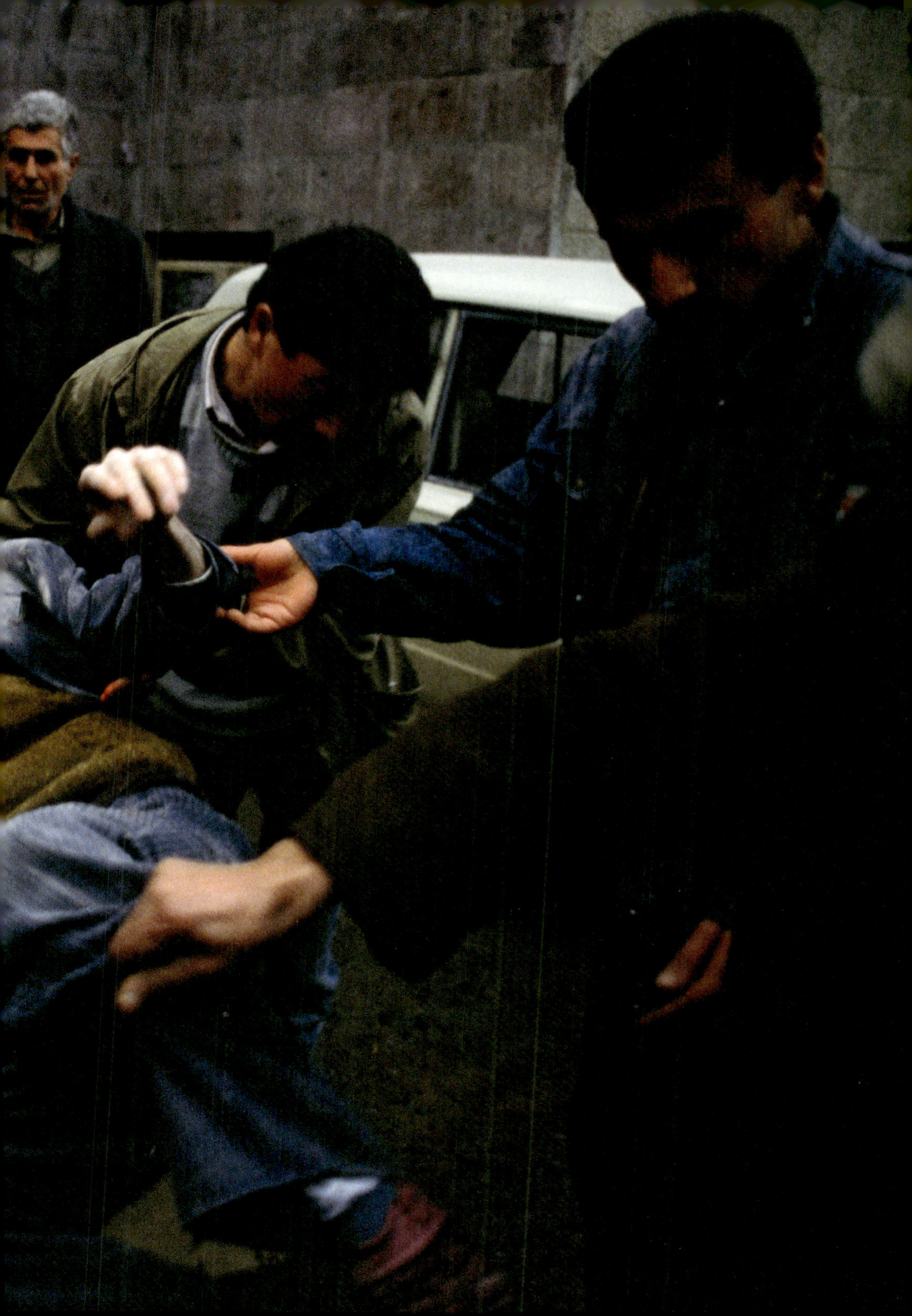

I first saw war in Nagorno-Karabakh, a mountainous region in the Caucasus disputed by Armenia and Azerbaijan. I departed from Kiev—where I'd been living for several months—with a crew comprised of Askold, Dima, and Natalya. Askold, an English-Ukrainian correspondent, was an old Afghan war hand, convinced of his lucky star. He asked me to accompany him on an assignment for his newspaper, *The European*, reassuring me that in all his years on the front he had "never had a scratch," and that everything would be fine—a comment that in time I learned to mean exactly the opposite. Dima, an extremely thin Armenian activist who lived in Ukraine and Canada, was our guide and very nervous. As for Natalya, a flame-headed former Soviet volleyball star, I never understood what she was doing with us, but she smiled a lot and that somehow made me feel better.

We left Kiev on a midnight flight to the Armenian capital, Yerevan, arriving in a city with little heat or electricity. We walked up eight flights of stairs to the apartment of Dima's wife—the lift had not been working for more than a year—and slept fully clothed for a few hours before returning to the airport to look for a helicopter flying into Nagorno-Karabakh.

There was only one helicopter making the trip that day, a grimy, knackered Soviet Mi-8. We arrived to find it surrounded by a mass of beings and objects, including a barrel of petrol, boxes of rifles, and several cages filled with chickens—obviously far more than could possibly fit on board. Sensing a delicate situation, we sent Dima to negotiate. This turned out to be a mistake, for Dima was an intellectual and preferred the power of ideas over money, an approach the pilot found unconvincing. Just as our predicament seemed hopeless, Askold, comprehending the desperation of the moment, sacrificed—not without some bitterness—his only bottle of whiskey. A few minutes later, we were airborne. When we arrived inside Armenian-controlled Karabakh, we were met by a car and were driven ten kilometres to an abandoned school, which had become the headquarters of a small unit of irregular troops. I had expected to find highly trained soldiers, but these men were nonchalant and disorganised volunteers—one was an artist, another a dentist—drawn from across Armenian society. The next morning, they took us to their position opposite an Azeri village, which they then started mortaring without any discernible purpose. This lasted for about thirty minutes until they ran out of shells, whereupon a heavy machine gun opened fire on us, pinning us motionless for three hours. I lay nose in the ground behind a small berm of earth, struggling to grasp the fact that if I stood up I would be killed. My bewilderment was interrupted only by Askold asking, with the air of a man who had become lost in some quaint part of the British countryside, if I had by any chance brought some sandwiches: ham or ham and cheese, he added, he wasn't fussy. I had not. When the firing eventually stopped, we crawled away until it felt safe enough to stand up and walk back to the school.

I went on patrol with these soldiers for the next two days, but little happened, so we decided to head to the capital of Nagorno-Karabakh, Stepanakert, which was then controlled by Armenian forces but was under siege from Azeri guns in the hills above. Shells were raining on the city as we arrived and we ditched the car, feeling safer on foot. We hugged the walls of buildings as shrapnel shredded the air, but I kept stopping, transfixed by the whistling sound of the shards of metal flying past us. During a lull in the bombardment, we arrived at a hospital where, like a macabre object of installation art, canvas stretchers stained ketchup-red with dollops of fresh blood were propped up against

First Blood

Nagorno-Karabakh, South Caucasus
16 February 1992

the wall. I wandered the hospital's darkened corridors, stumbling into an operating theatre at the precise moment a shell struck the building. Everyone, including the surgeons, ran to the sides of the room, leaving the wounded patient on the table as chunks of plaster fell from the ceiling and the walls shook like jelly. Another shell landed, and I felt sure that the room would collapse in on us. Then, suddenly, there was silence. At first, I was frozen to the spot; only when it became clear that the shelling had stopped was I able to move again. I ran back to the entrance to find Askold and the others, who were calmly standing outside smoking cigarettes.

A stream of cars screeched into the hospital yard, bearing wounded civilians from the recent barrage. Askold leapt forwards to open their doors, like a doorman from one of London's better hotels, as hysterical relatives grabbed the first stretcher they could find and carried the wounded inside. All the time I was taking pictures in Nagorno-Karabakh, I assumed that the extraordinary scenes all around me were being captured vividly on my films. In fact, because of my inexperience, what I saw and what I photographed were two distant relatives, although I was to find this out only weeks later, when my slides were processed. This photograph, showing a wounded, elderly man arriving at the hospital, was alone in capturing any measure of the violence I saw.

I remember chasing this man into the corridor, as if that were the obvious thing to be doing, before returning to the entrance and stopping to catch my breath. I felt as if I were drowning on dry land, or falling off a cliff. When I gripped the camera and looked through the lens, I found I could concentrate, as if its tunnel vision isolated me from the chaos. But the moment I put it down I was overwhelmed by the sensation of being so close to the threshold between life and death. This, of course, was what I had come to witness. And yet my distance from the emotional pain that accompanied it made me realise that I was also an intruder, and that the mantle of a photojournalist was far less comfortable to wear than I had ever imagined. The following afternoon, there was calm in Stepanakert and we returned to the group of irregulars with whom we had started our stay in Nagorno-Karabakh. Here were people I recognized. I felt glad to be with them again, and safer, too, despite my doubts about their soldiering. When we arrived, they were preparing their weapons and equipment for a night operation.

The next morning, I woke up early to find them safely back and sitting by the fire with a prisoner. Clearly, they hadn't been expecting to see me. As I approached, half of them stood up and took the prisoner, who began kicking and screaming, behind a wooden hut a short distance away. I sat there with the others as they stared intently at the fire, pretending that nothing was happening. Two minutes later, the first group of soldiers returned with the prisoner's head. There was no attempt to hide it, or perhaps they believed that somehow I was on their side and therefore complicit with their actions. I felt entirely betrayed. When I asked why they had done this—people with whom I had shared the bond of being in danger together, even bandaging a wounded soldier together—they looked at me as if I had lost my way. He had tortured their comrades, they told me. This was the punishment, and also the end of the conversation. They placed the head in a muslin bag and deposited it inside the back of a red Lada parked by the school entrance—the same car that, two hours later, took us to a helicopter flying to Yerevan. All the way to the heliport on that bumpy road, I pretended to ignore the sound of that head rattling around in the boot of the car. Perhaps that has made its existence all the more difficult to forget.

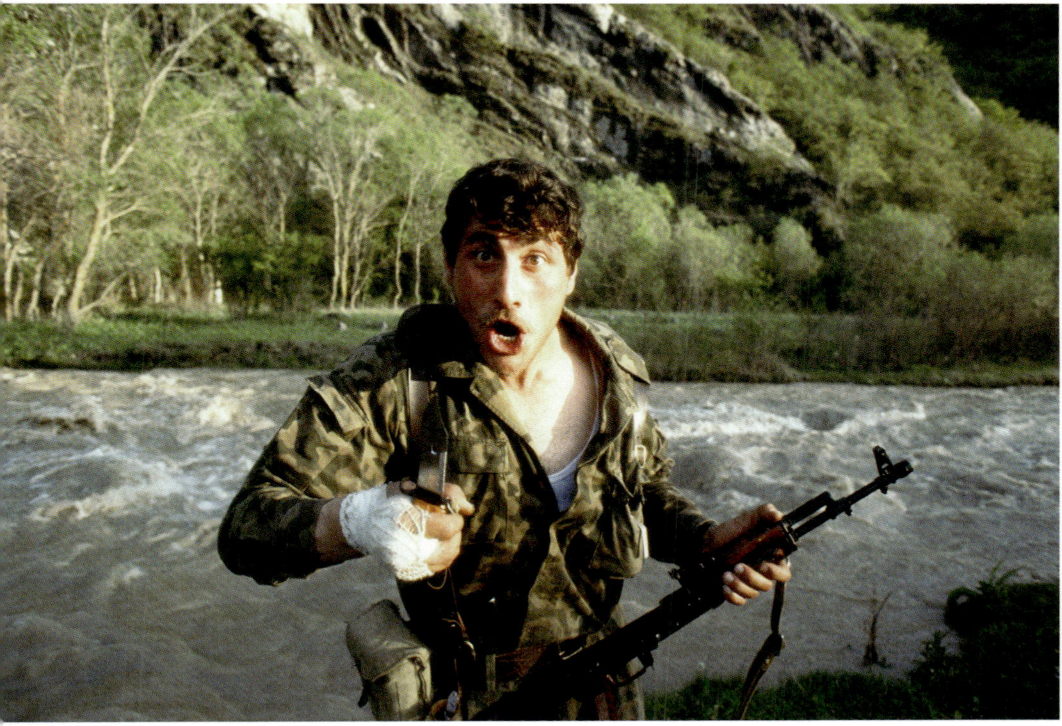

Georgian hospitality is legendary throughout the Caucasus. A friend of mine was once pursued across the capital, Tbilisi, by a car filled with crazed men who he assumed were out to rob him. After a furious chase, they cut him off in a cul-de-sac and leapt out of their car and into his—only to invite him to lunch. Refusing such offers is impossible, as I found out with my friend Zanny, a budding journalist who had persuaded me to travel through Georgia with her.

It all began over breakfast at the Intourist hotel in Gori, in central Georgia. We were staring out the window at the famous mud house where Stalin had been born, ignoring our sausage and eggs, when a ragtag group of soldiers entered the restaurant bearing an enormous flagon of wine bound in straw. After stacking their Kalashnikovs against the wall, the soldiers proceeded to pass around the flagon even before their food arrived. And when they spotted the two foreigners in the room—one of them a pretty blonde—arguments against joining their table were useless. There was more than enough wine for all of us.

Zanny and I knew that a civil war was simmering between the Georgian central government and separatist forces in South Ossetia, an autonomous republic just to the north; these soldiers, we learned, had returned from patrol only that morning, and they regaled us with tales of their escapades. As it happened, they intended to head back again later in the day, after receiving fresh orders from their commander.

At the time, I spoke almost no Russian. Still, after a few more stories and passes of the bottle, the possibility of returning with these soldiers to the front began to seem like an excellent idea: unfettered access to the war without official permission from Tbilisi was almost unobtainable. The soldiers agreed—at this point in our quickly blooming friendship, they probably would have agreed to anything—and it was decided that we would meet up again at midday outside the hotel restaurant to begin the journey to the front.

Zanny and I had been standing on the pavement for more than an hour when the soldiers rolled up in a pair of jeeps and announced that the plan had changed: their commanding officer was stuck in the capital, and so they had decided to have a picnic instead. It would be a great honour if such dignified British guests would accompany them. Zanny and I climbed in.

To my concern, we were soon heading east on the road to Tbilisi, and I worried that our new friends might be planning to turn us over to the authorities. Instead we pulled over at a bus stop, where a stormy conversation erupted between the captain and two prostitutes who were standing on the side of the road. After five

The Drunken Picnic

Gori, Georgia
18 May 1992

minutes of this ferocious exchange—though pretty much any conversation in Georgian sounds ferocious—the women reluctantly wedged themselves in the back of our jeep, and we turned back towards Gori. After a brief detour to the market to buy meat and fruit and even more wine—although God knows how much we had already consumed by this point—we headed south to the hills beyond Gori, winding through a series of ravines until we halted in an open field next to a wide, fast-flowing river.

The captain switched on the radio in one of the jeeps. Two soldiers served cups filled to the brim with wine. Two other soldiers cut up meat with their bayonets as the lieutenant started a fire. Then the men—officers first—took turns disappearing into the bushes with the two women, who welcomed, in turn, all six of them, pausing only when the meat was cooked and we all sat down to eat.

After lunch, we danced and fired Kalashnikovs. The soldiers thrust the weapons into our arms and, whether we wanted to or not, Zanny and I shot at the cliffs across the river as if they were our mortal enemies.

As the light started to fade, one of the soldiers went to clean his rifle next to the river, and I followed. Suddenly, he picked up his bayonet and thrust it at me, roaring, and I snapped this picture. The next minute, he was laughing—it was all a big joke—but I probably would have been scared if I hadn't been far too drunk to feel much of anything.

When I look at this photograph, the folly of that afternoon is eclipsed by an overwhelming sense of sorrow. After the Soviet Union collapsed, ethnic tensions that had lain dormant in the Caucasus for decades flared up. Neighbours and friends became enemies overnight, and soldiers like this one, often unprepared for combat but full of patriotic fervour, set out for the front. Perhaps this young man survived, but the world he grew up in has disappeared. Twenty years later, the fate of a nominally independent South Ossetia, where he was fighting, remains unclear—even after a second war, and the loss of thousands of lives.

It was dark by the time everyone was sated and we returned to Gori. At the hotel, there was a huge wedding banquet in progress, and the receptionist informed us that we were invited to join the festivities—by now, news of the two British guests had spread far and wide. We tried to tiptoe unnoticed past the open door of the restaurant but, alas, a sharp-eyed relative spotted us and we were captured. For the next two hours, we ate and drank more than seemed humanly possible, making endless toasts to the newlyweds and to happiness in general.

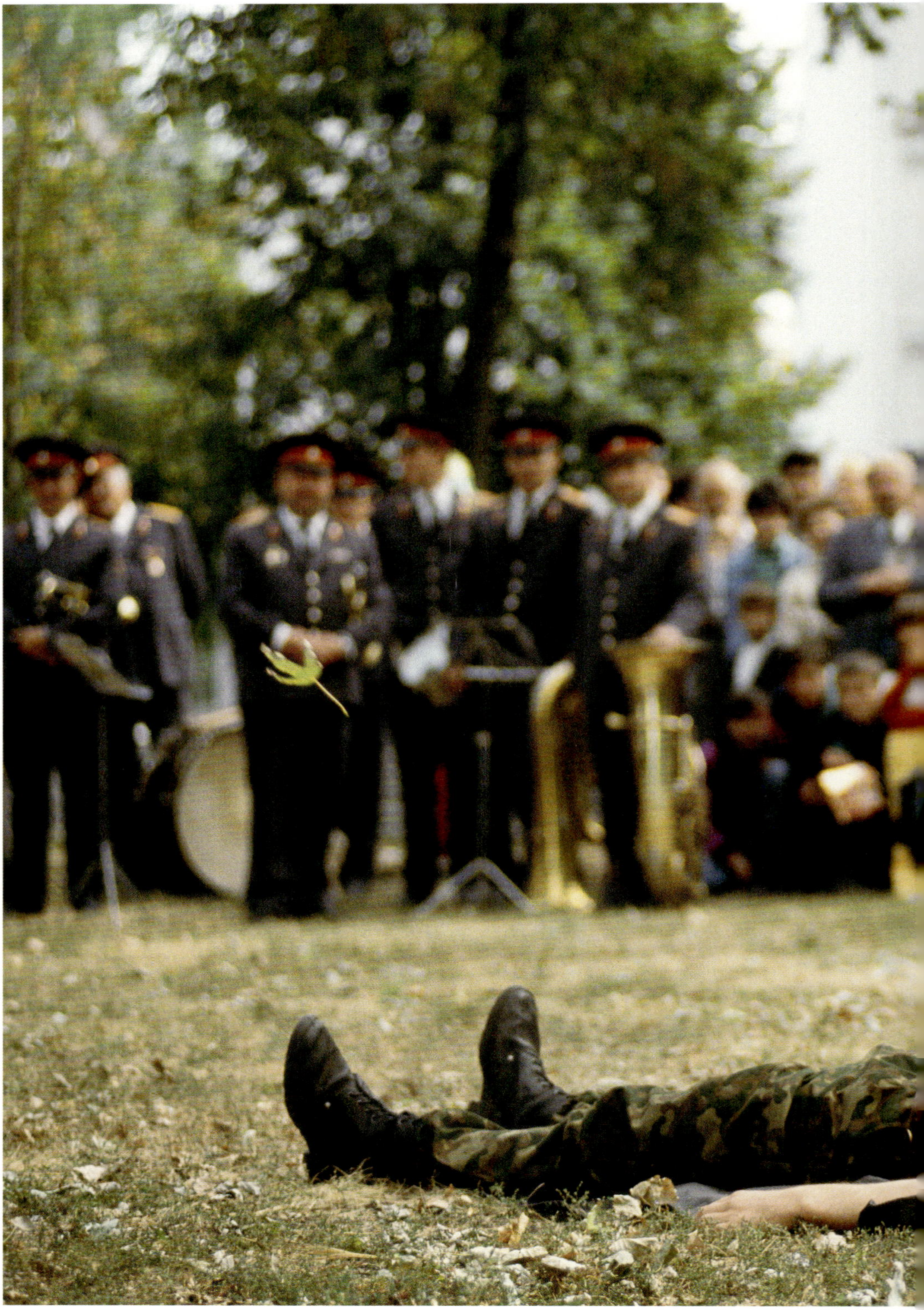

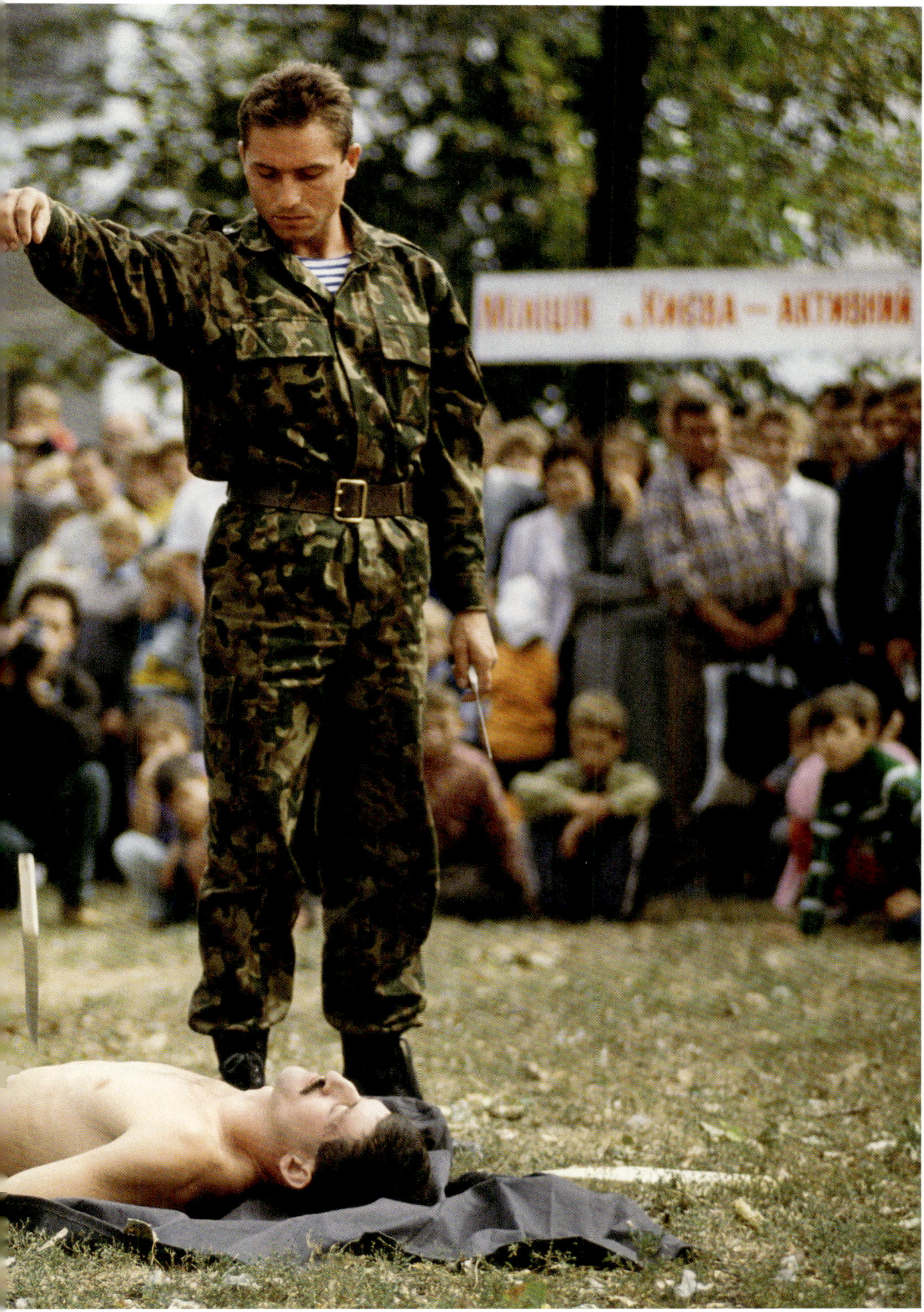
Міліція „Києва — АКТИВНИЙ

When I left London for Kiev, the capital of Ukraine, in October 1991, I was carrying two cameras, four lenses, and sixty rolls of colour-negative film. The film had been given to me by the photo editor of *The Times*—the only editor from the London papers who had agreed to meet with me before I disappeared to the Soviet Union. He patted me on the back and told me to send pictures from time to time, rather in the way a commander would say farewell to a soldier on a dangerous mission, assuming that he would never see him again.

Originally, I had hoped to go to Moscow; the collapse of the Berlin Wall and events in Eastern Europe seemed to presage something dramatic in the Soviet capital. But getting a Russian visa proved impossible, and instead I went to Kiev after a chance meeting with a British journalist based in Ukraine who agreed, in a moment of weakness, to put me up for a few months.

Despite an exterior of bravado, I wasn't too optimistic about my prospects. Although I told my friends in London that I was departing on a great adventure—which was true—I didn't believe it would be more than six months before I returned to England in search of more traditional employment. Already I had used up most of my savings to buy the two cameras, a Nikon F3 and a Leica M6 rangefinder, in the vain hope that the mere possession of these instruments would help transform me into a real photojournalist. As I subsequently learned in Nagorno-Karabakh, however, they did not.

Instead it was the Soviet Union that saved me. Not only was it fascinating, offering a vast array of stories, but the Soviet economy made me rich. Thanks to the

The Golden Eagles

Kiev
September 1992

insatiable black-market demand for dollars, whose exchange rate outstripped the official one, I was able to live and work in a way far beyond my wildest expectations. To fly from Kiev to Moscow with Aeroflot cost only fifty cents. Even travelling to several of the republics of the Soviet Union and staying each night in hotels, I was hard-pressed to spend more than five hundred dollars a month—which was just as well, since I was barely making more than that. As for the food shortage, which was very real that first winter—I once kept a taxi waiting for forty minutes after I spotted a man selling Cuban grapefruits in the street—years of English school canteens had taught me how to survive on any diet imaginable, which in those early months consisted almost entirely of vodka, cigarettes, potatoes, and pickled cucumbers.

Then I had another stroke of luck. On Christmas Day 1991, Mikhail Gorbachev officially dissolved the Soviet Union. Ukraine—a country the size of France and armed with nuclear weapons—became a very big story. Editors who had previously ignored my calls suddenly became interested in my photographs. Although Kiev boasted plenty of talented local photographers, almost none of them could speak English; those who did already worked for the international wire agencies, effectively making me the obvious choice for international assignments.

The only impediment to working in Ukraine was getting the films out of the country. I shot nearly all my work on slide film, but there were no laboratories in Kiev to develop it. International couriers were forbidden to ship unprocessed film, and I had to beg diplomats and friends to carry bags of film, arranging for them to be met at airports in London, Paris, New York, or wherever.

I was also able to sell my photo stories to magazines. Editors were curious to see almost any material offered, because so few Western photographers had had open access during the Soviet era, and they seemed particularly entranced by anything military. In my experience, neither editors nor photographers are very good at resisting clichés; so when I got a call from the Ministry of the Interior, inviting me to a demonstration by their newly formed Special Operations Group, the Golden Eagles, I decided to go along.

The soldiers started with some easy stuff, mostly mock hand-to-hand fighting, just to get the crowd warmed up. Then they moved into the showy numbers—punching bricks and chopping planks with their bare hands, smashing bottles on their uncovered heads.

The spectators, in a state of astonishment and unsure what could possibly top the previous displays, drew a collective breath when one of the soldiers pulled a dagger from its scabbard. His colleague then stripped to the waist and lay on the ground, holding a block of wood over his stomach. The soldier dropped his knife, letting it plunge into the wood with a resonating twang. The supine soldier then removed the block and visibly clenched his stomach muscles. The crowd tensed with him. And the knife dropped once more—passing, by chance, a leaf floating gently to the ground—before it miraculously bounced off the soldier's stomach, prompting a furious round of applause.

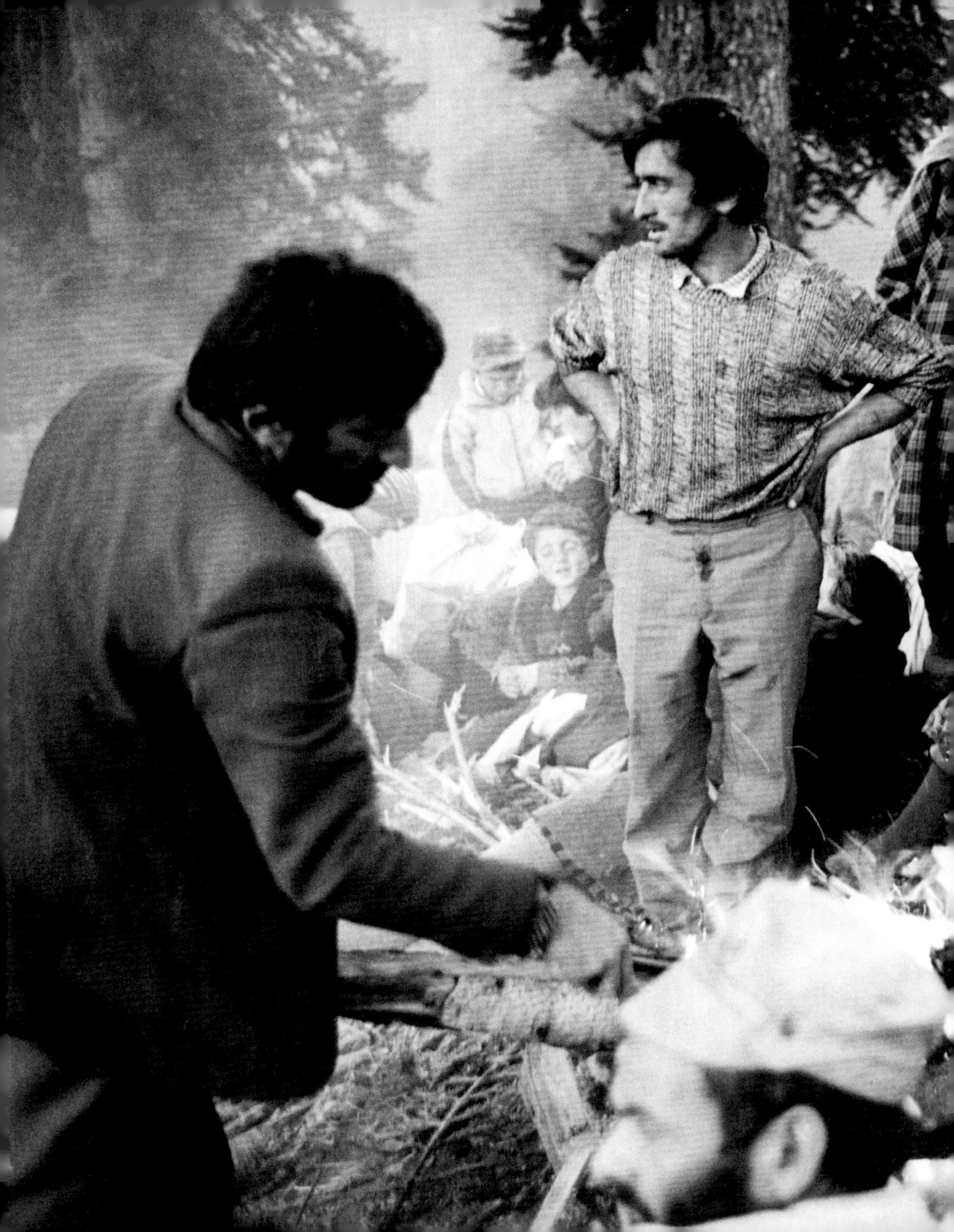

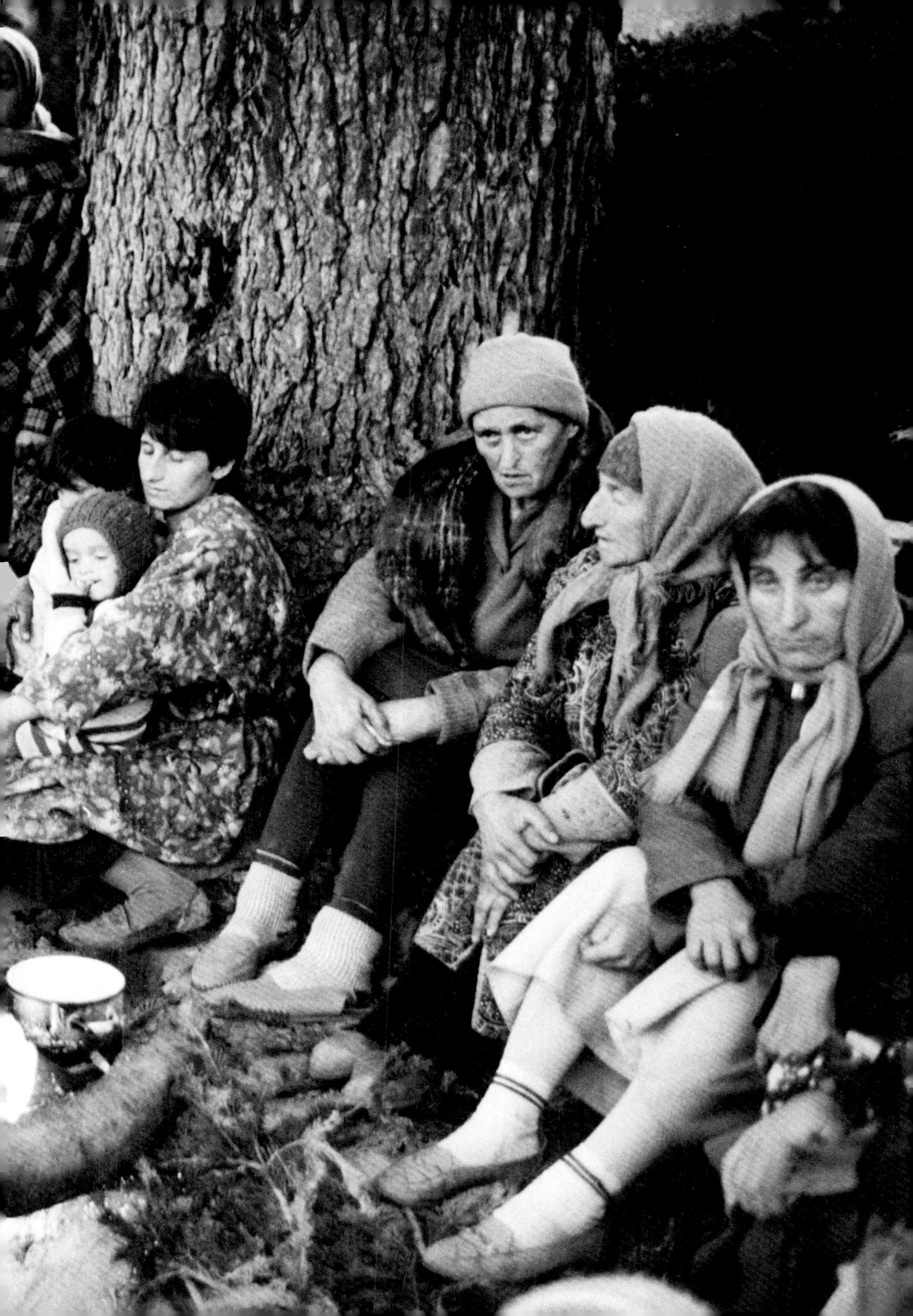

The battle for Sukhumi was the decisive victory in Abkhazia's separatist revolt against Georgia. When it ended and Abkhaz forces stood triumphant in the city's ruins, the Georgian government troops fled in panic, with tens of thousands of ethnic Georgians in their wake. The refugees who were fast, or lucky, escaped to central Georgia by the main highway across the Inguri River, the disputed border between the two republics. After rebel forces captured that road, however, the only route to safety for the Georgians still trapped inside Abkhazia was a fearsome trek north across the Caucasus Mountains.

I arrived in the Georgian capital, Tbilisi, just as this exodus was beginning, three hundred and fifty kilometres to the west. I joined forces with two other photographers, and together we persuaded the presidential press attaché to find us a way to Abkhazia. The next morning, the four of us boarded a Soviet-era Mi-8 helicopter taking supplies to the refugees.

After lifting off, we first headed west to the town of Kutaisi, in central Georgia, where a lone bread truck stood waiting for us on the airport's deserted runway. We jumped out of the helicopter so that the driver and his burly mate could stash their hundreds of loaves in the cabin; then we climbed back in and wedged ourselves against a wall of warm bread.

An hour later, we crossed the border into Abkhazia. The helicopter landed at the foot of the mountains in an area thick with pine trees, and we quickly disembarked. The ground was littered with people and possessions, and the refugees' desperation was palpable. The pilot kept the rotors whirring as the loaves were thrown into a sea of clamouring hands, and then, without consulting us, he took off again, fearing for his aircraft's safety.

This was not a possibility I had prepared for. All I had with me were my cameras and the clothes I was wearing. I looked at the refugees, who regarded me with equal curiosity: after all, we had just gone to great lengths to arrive in the very place they were trying to escape. The only thing we shared was our predicament. Behind us was the road to the coast and their enemies; ahead, a path over the towering mountains. Already, artifacts from the refugees' past lives were scattered around me: cars, carpets, televisions, everything too heavy to take with them. Then, only a few hundred metres on, lay the more intimate and precious treasures and mementos; within minutes, these family albums and toys had also become too burdensome and been abandoned in the mud.

At first, the path seemed easy. We wove our way up through majestic pines, following a trail trodden down by thousands of feet. But then evening fell and we stopped short of the tree line, deciding to take shelter in the forest against the cold night ahead. Pascal and Mike, the two experienced photographers, had brought sleeping bags with them. Vata, the presidential press attaché, and I had nothing except each other to keep warm; as the temperature plummeted, we cuddled like spoons but even so were soon shivering uncontrollably. Only by jumping up and down to warm ourselves could we then rest a few minutes before the cold began gnawing at us once more. And so we jumped and paused, jumped and paused, until we saw the blessed break of day and walked out, exhausted, to warm ourselves in the sun's first rays.

Once we were above the forest, the climb became even steeper. Many of the refugees had already been out of their homes for a week, without a bed or much to eat, and the weakest soon began to fail. At first, just a few corpses littered the ground, then more and more

The Long March

Abkhazian-Georgian Border
October 1993

abandoned where they fell, since no one had a spade or the strength to pierce the frozen ground and bury them.

As the sun rose higher, we came across an old man sitting on an enormous jam jar. He was wearing a woollen cap, and his face was thick with silvery stubble. His watery eyes, for some reason, fixed on me, and even before he spoke a word I knew that his family had left him behind. We were four young men; he begged us to carry him. We listened—he spoke Russian, not Georgian, so I understood him—but guilt has made me forget what we replied before we turned to the mountain and walked away. That stare still wakes me in the middle of the night. Ever since, I have been trying to excuse myself for leaving him there.

Of course, there are always excuses. We wouldn't have had the strength to carry him more than a hundred metres. I found myself remembering the story of a photographer who had travelled with the Kurds in 1991 when they fled their homes in northern Iraq as Saddam Hussein sought vengeance at the end of the first Gulf War. The photographer had become so exhausted during the trek that he abandoned his cameras, saving only his films. When I had read this story, just a few months earlier, I couldn't imagine how a photographer could become so tired that he would throw away thousands of dollars' worth of cameras. And yet here I was, gasping for breath in the thin air and struggling to put one foot in front of the other. Nevertheless, that old man's face, in its last hours of life, has never left me.

We climbed, it seemed, forever, deceived by false crests, and just as we believed that we would never reach the pass we suddenly stood at the top, staring down into Georgia. Men and women lay all around us on the ground, soaking in the afternoon sun, unable to believe that, physically, the hardest part was behind them. An hour later, with renewed strength, we started the walk down. In the cover of the tree line, hundreds of refugees were camped around makeshift fires, and in this photograph you can see their emotional and physical exhaustion. Young and old together, they sat with their only remaining possessions: their clothes and their lives.

That night, we cut up our last food: a Mars bar and a tin of cod-liver pâté. Pascal sliced the bar with his penknife, attempting surgeon-like strokes to make perfect quarters as we watched, our hungry stares making him nervous.

Just after dawn, we began the descent with the mass of refugees. Supposedly, somewhere below us, there was a collection point from which helicopters were ferrying refugees to Kutaisi—the same airport where we had stopped for bread only a few days before. Each time we asked how far there was to go, the answer was a distance longer than the last.

We reached the collection point at dusk. We found huge crowds swarming three helicopters, while the pilots attempted in vain to organise them. The refugees tried every trick to get onboard, throwing babies in the air and exhorting frail pensioners to weep. Ten helicopters came and left before we managed to force our way on, too. The craft was so laden that the rotors were barely able to lift us into the thin mountain air, and it seemed an eternity before the ground finally fell away beneath us.

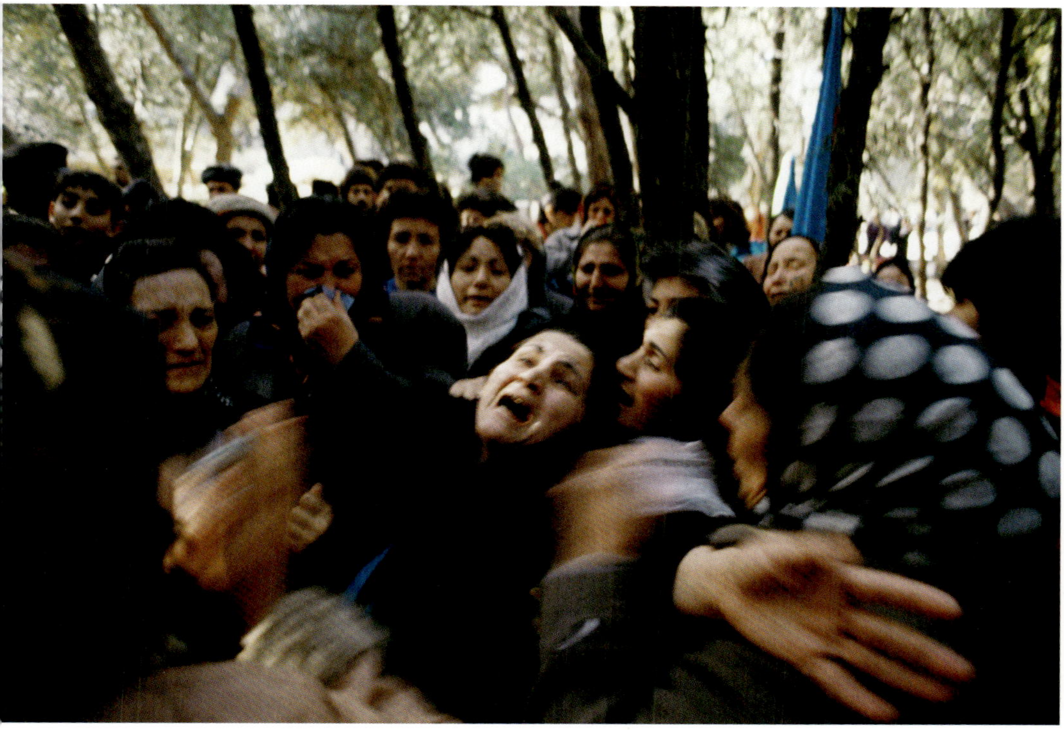

The Lost Son

Martyrs' Lane, Baku, Azerbaijan
November 1993

During the bitter conflict between Azerbaijan and Armenia over Nagorno-Karabakh, on any given day in the winter of 1993 you could walk up to Martyrs' Lane, the cemetery high above the Caspian shore in the Azeri capital, Baku, and find a mother burying her son.

Sure enough, as I wandered among the pine-shaded graves one morning, I found a lone man at work preparing the resting place for a soldier. As I arrived, he was carefully scraping the last shovels of earth from the grave.

It wasn't long before I heard the distinctive sound of Chopin's funeral march being played, quite awfully, by a brass band. Then I saw a procession approaching from the direction of the cemetery's entrance, led by a man in a suit bearing a black-and-white portrait of a smiling young soldier. A black ribbon ran diagonally across one corner of the frame. Next came the pallbearers, carrying the coffin shoulder high, and then the soldier's sobbing mother, barely able to keep the pace.

The funeral party took several minutes to reach me by the graveside, and when the mother came close enough to look into the deep hole she broke down completely, throwing her arms into the air as if to ask God why He had chosen her son to die.

There were no other photographers or cameramen that day to mark the burial of this ordinary soldier. Despite the mourners' unspoken acquiescence in, even approval of, my decision to record the proceedings, I was unable to banish the awkward sense of being an uninvited guest. Nor was I able to dismiss the discomfort of photographing what for me has always been the most painful of griefs—that of a mother who has lost a child.

The mourners gathered around the graveside and a mullah read verses from the Koran. The pallbearers lowered the coffin into the ground. As they did so, all eyes turned towards the mother, who clawed at her face, gouging bloody tracks down her cheeks. Like the chorus of a Greek tragedy, her female relatives wailed in unison as, one by one, friends and family members shuffled past the grave, picking up a handful of earth to throw over the coffin. When they had finished, the gravedigger piled the remaining earth over the grave, smoothing a mound with the back of his shovel and arranging heaps of red carnations upon it.

As soon as he had done so, the funeral came to an abrupt end. The mother stopped wailing and turned her back on the grave, as if she had no more emotions to release. The funeral party descended the hill back to the road. And then, when the mourners were almost out of sight, the gravedigger began his work again.

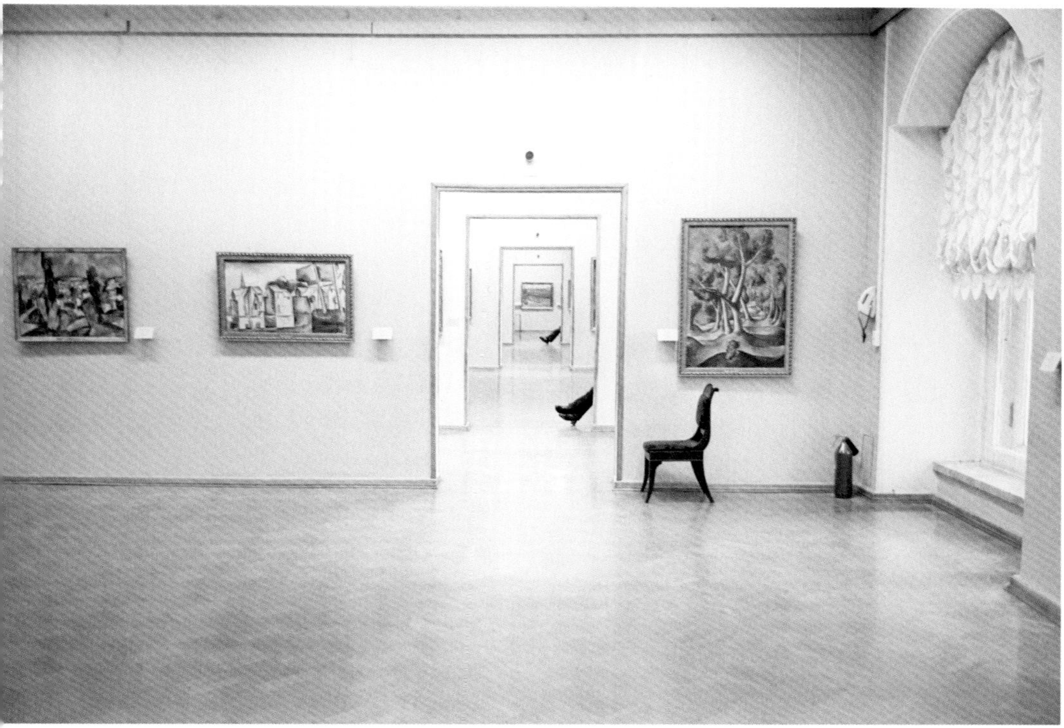

Watching

The Hermitage Museum, St. Petersburg

November 1994

The old Russian women who guard the endless corridors of The Hermitage have always unnerved me. Even when I'm not standing too close to the masterpiece on the wall, their surveillance has invariably made me feel guilty.

There is no escaping them, for they are everywhere: wandering the palace's gilded halls, glaring out from the grille of the ticket office, taking your coat at the cloakroom—usually hoping to complain that the hook at the back of your collar is broken—before allowing you, grudgingly, to enter their kingdom.

Boundless, crammed with masterpieces, The Hermitage is an enormous maze, a place outside time. On some visits, I lose myself in the sixteenth-century European paintings; on others, I visit the Scythian treasure or attempt—often without success—to find the Malachite Room. When rushed, I may choose a single painting—Rembrandt's "Return of the Prodigal Son," Matisse's "Dance"—and just look, letting my eyes roam until I find a new detail that I had somehow missed. It is like discovering something about a familiar acquaintance that I had never registered before.

Photographers are often drawn to museums, for nowhere else is the art of looking more refined. I love to watch the visitors roam the grand expanses and to notice what catches their eye. Then I turn back to the canvases themselves and think about what first caught the eye of those who painted them, and the way each generation of artists has chosen to frame the world around them.

On the second floor of the museum, where this photograph was taken, the rooms are too low for the lustrous chandeliers of the piano nobile; instead, they are softly illuminated by the gentle light filtering through the netted windows overlooking Alexander Square, where ant-size pedestrians roam the vast space below. Against the plain walls, the riotous succession of Impressionist and Post-Impressionist paintings, hanging in room after room, seems almost shocking.

On this particular day, the tide of tourists usually flooding this floor had mysteriously receded, leaving the galleries unnaturally still; the only people on view were two partially obscured guards. The first one, I noted, was wearing a pair of Cuban-heeled boots.

I took just one picture. And even though I was carrying the most discreet of cameras—a Leica rangefinder—I imagined the first guard glaring at me through the wall, infuriated by the barely audible click of the shutter. Surely, she could not have witnessed my transgression. Nevertheless, I moved gingerly on, treading tentatively on the parquet, praying that it would not creak.

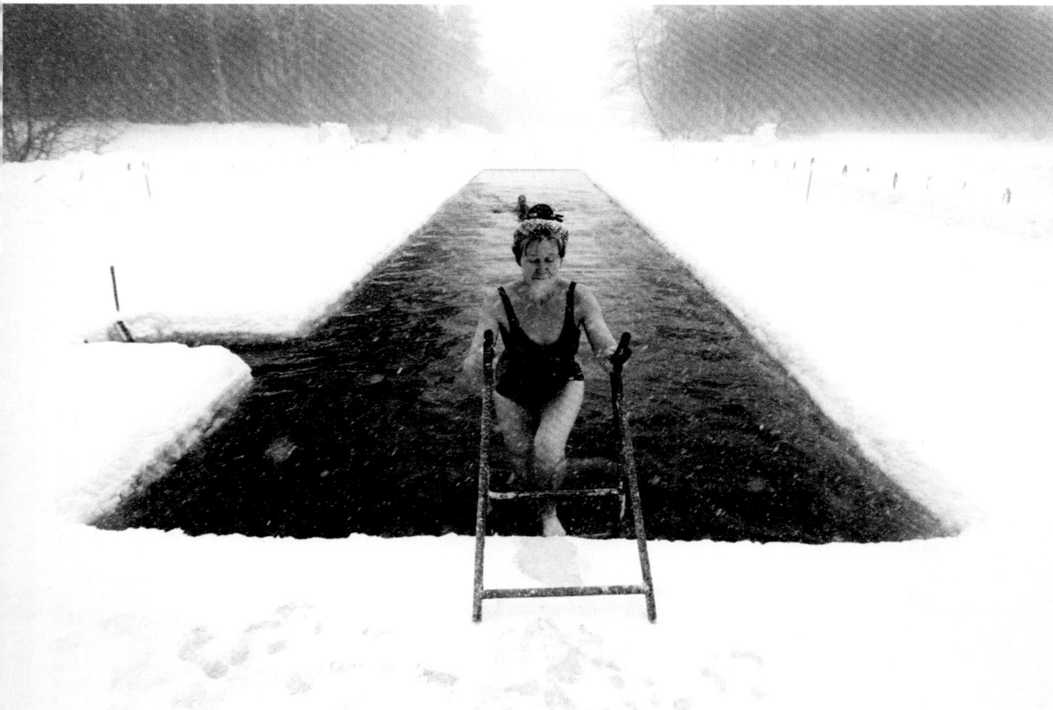

The Walrus

Silver Woods, Moscow
17 February 1996

Walruses, as the winter swimmers are known in Russia, invariably try to convert you. When they ask if you have been baptised, they do not mean in the ecclesiastical sense. They are merely daring you to shed your heavy coat and plunge in.

In Moscow, walruses can often be spotted in the Silver Woods, on the western edge of the Russian capital. There, nestled between tall pine trees, lies a picturesque lake that is home to the Moscow Walrus Club.

At the beginning of the winter, the club members carve themselves a rectangular pool in the ice. Each Saturday morning, they return to the lake bearing enormous saws to cut through the new ice that has formed during the week. They push the larger blocks of ice under the sides and fish out the smaller pieces with a bamboo pole, leaving the water a gleaming strip of black.

Retiring to the hut to change, they slip into their bathing suits. Then, without fussing or flesh-pounding, they calmly step into the icy water as if it were the most natural thing to be doing on a winter's day.

Some swim for ten minutes. Others simply go to the end and back. But on the morning that I visited, one woman stood out amongst the intrepid bathers. She was a delicate but nimble babushka, the quintessential Russian grandmother, and she swam six lengths of the pool with a precise and measured breaststroke. So smoothly did she glide from one end of the pool to the other that the falling snow nestled in her hair. When she finally stepped out, there was a look of utter serenity on her face, as if she were exiting the swimming pool of a luxurious hotel on the Côte d'Azur rather than an icy lake in Moscow. And then, barefoot, she returned to the hut to change.

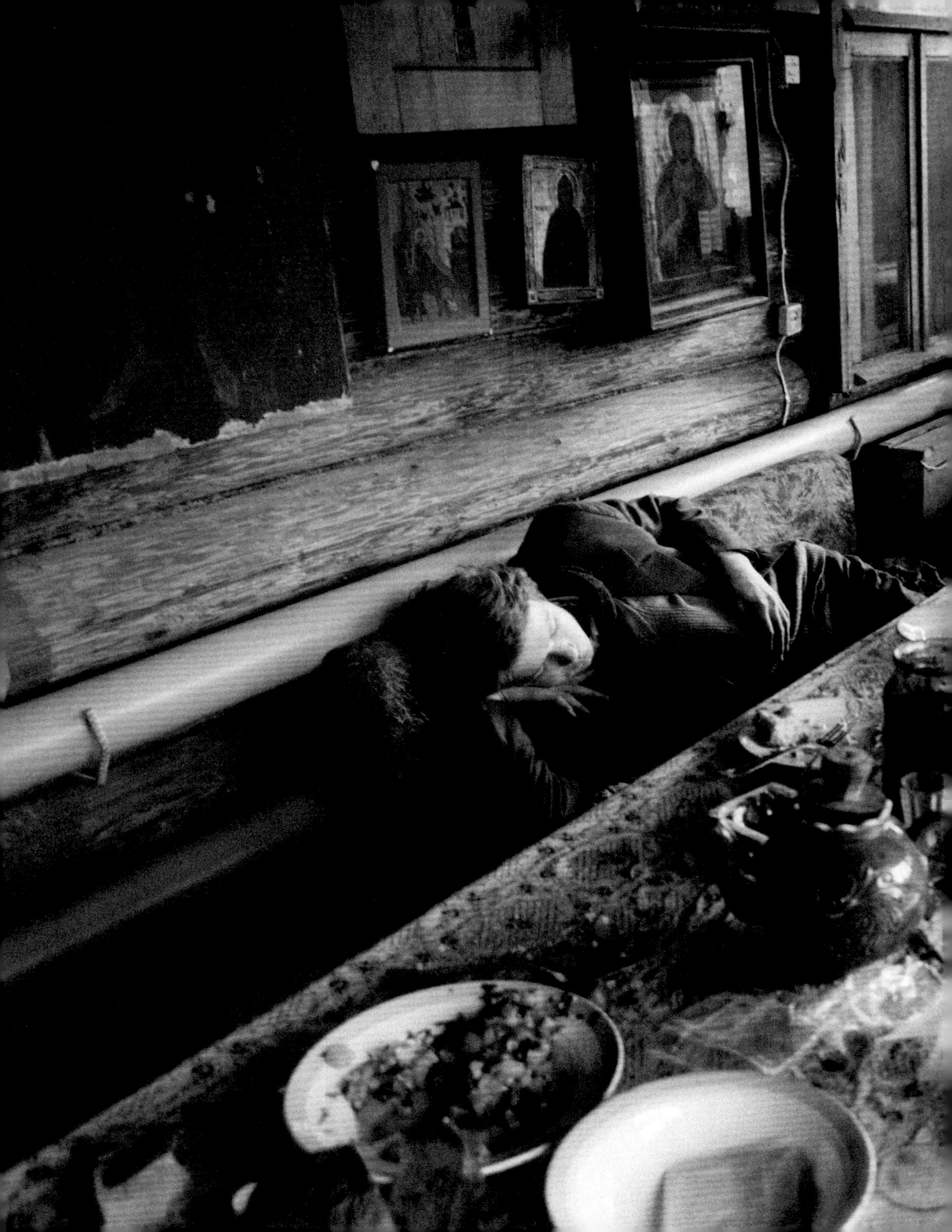

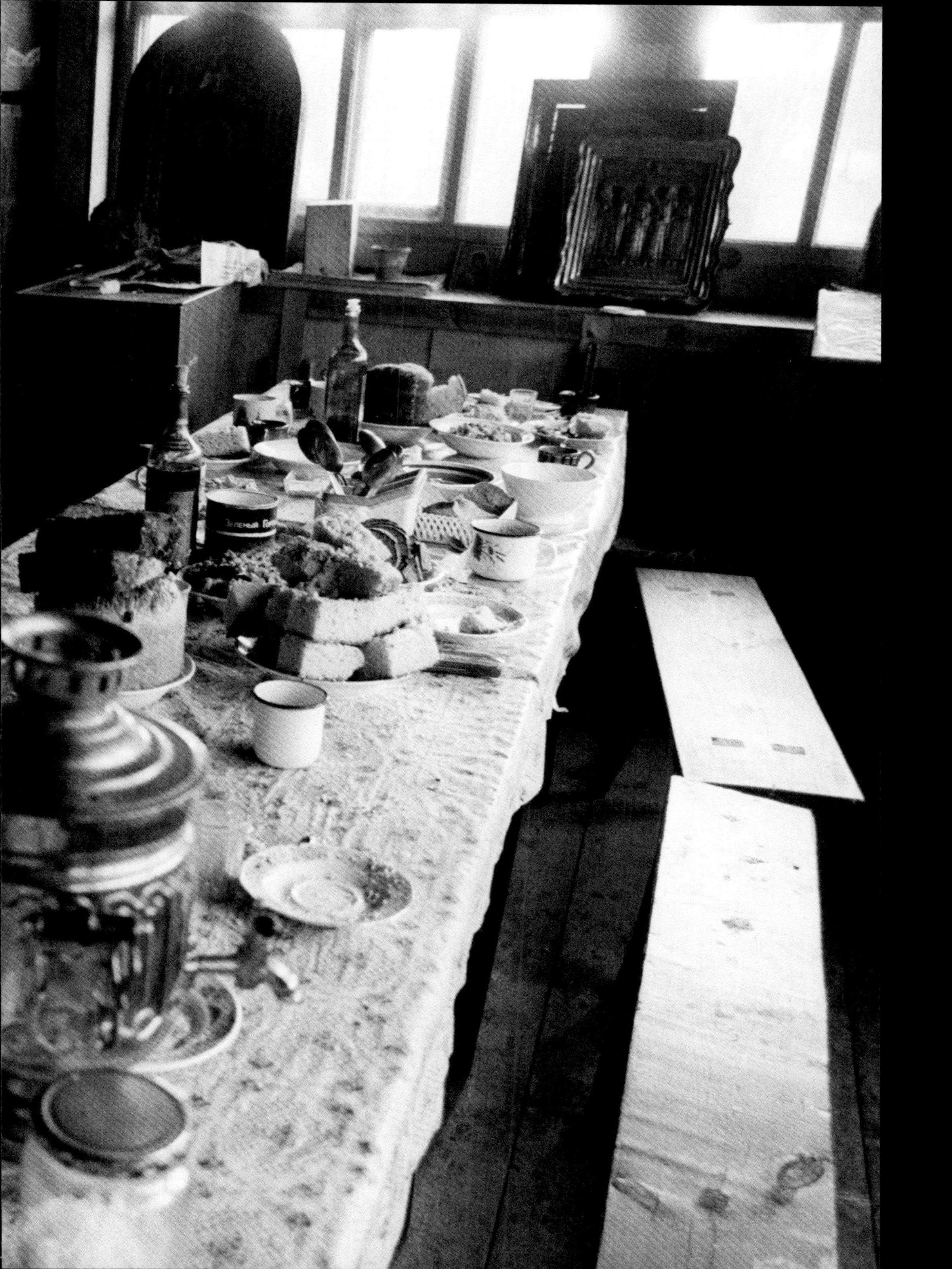
Зеленый

The Morning After the Night Before

Easter, Tver Region, Russia
27 April 1997

My diary for that week offers few clues about this picture. There are no names or places, just three words, "Russian Orthodox Easter." Before and after, the days are blank, as if they had been swallowed up into the past without a trace.

My friend Dmitri had persuaded me to spend Easter with him, as a guest of a priest he knew in the Tver region, five hours north of Moscow by car. On Saturday morning, I collected Dmitri from outside Moscow's Savelovsky Station in my battered red Toyota Corolla, its exhaust pipe sounding as though we might leave earth's orbit at any moment.

It was cold for late April and a thick mist hung over the fields as we drove north. The Russian winter, as usual, was refusing to release its grip. When we reached our destination, I wandered through the village, with curious eyes watching me from behind lace-curtained windows. I entered the church. There, as I moved from icon to icon, flustered ladies followed me, sweeping up the clumps of dried mud that I left trailing in my wake.

I stayed at the church all day, watching the preparations for the Easter Mass. The villagers began to arrive long before midnight, filling the nave and standing shoulder to shoulder, candles in one hand and baskets overflowing with coloured eggs and Easter cake in the other. The service went deep into the night, and it was very late when the priests finally retired to their quarters and invited us to join them for dinner, glad to break their Lenten fast with company. After this, however, I remember almost nothing.

Looking at this photograph, trying to re-enact the scenes that came before, I feel like a detective. I see all the usual suspects of a Russian village meal: a huge samovar for tea, honey cake, tins of peas, a bowl of buckwheat, slices of bread piled high and, this being Easter, kulich as well. There are bottles of vodka, as traditional with any village celebration. And after the toasts there must have been singing and laughter, but this is only guesswork. I know only that I took no photographs during the dinner. Perhaps the priests asked me to refrain; perhaps I simply felt it to be too intrusive.

From the contact sheets of my films, I can see that, after the Mass, I began to photograph again only in the early morning, when I found this young man asleep in the refectory. His identity remains a mystery, but it does not matter. Sometimes a photograph is only a hint, a souvenir of a forgotten moment—one of the thousands making up the jigsaw of our lives.

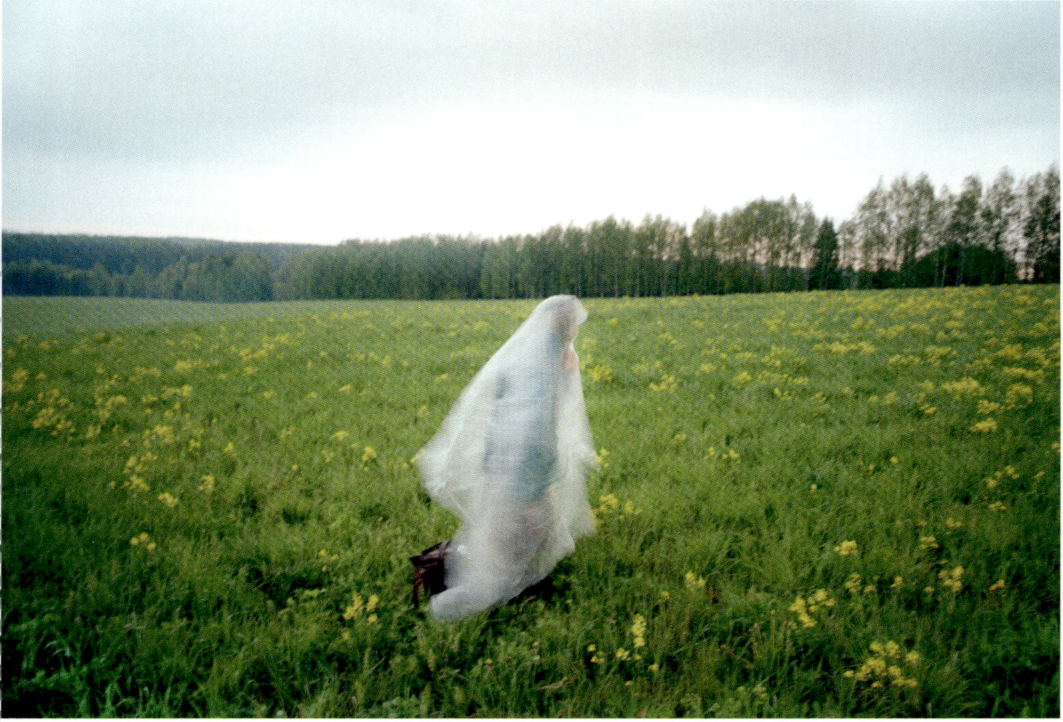

The Miracle Worker

Kirov Region, Russia
6 June 1997

Vladimir Syomin, the well-known Russian photographer, would often berate me for working on assignment, arguing that photography should be a mission rather than a profession, and that taking money compromised a photographer's vision. Mercifully, his artistic sanctity did not affect our friendship, and his home was as open to me as it was to any photographer living in Moscow or passing through it. One evening, I arrived for dinner and found the Czech photographer Josef Koudelka regaling a crowd of Russian colleagues with stories about the 1968 invasion of Czechoslovakia. We drank so much that night, however, that I remember little else.

Syomin's great love was the rural Russian Orthodox Church. Evidently worried about my creative well-being, he suggested that I accompany him on the Velikoretsky pilgrimage, which celebrates the discovery of an icon of St. Nicholas the Miracle Worker, in 1383.

The icon—a small wooden panel depicting scenes from the saint's life, with a gilded portrait at its centre—has always been thought to possess miraculous powers. It was first found by villagers in the depths of the Kirov region, northeast of Moscow, and donated to a church in the regional capital on the condition that it be returned to the village once a year. During the tsarist era, huge crowds gathered to accompany it home. Under the Communists, the pilgrimage was suppressed, only to be revived immediately after the collapse of the Soviet Union.

During four days in early June, Vladimir and I followed a procession of several thousand worshippers as it threaded its way across a hundred miles of idyllic countryside, framed by birch trees and fields of swaying rye. Our destination was the exact spot, on the banks of the River Veliky, where the icon had been found and where the pilgrims would soon baptise themselves, sending their prayers to St. Nicholas.

Although the pilgrims were of every age, a surprising number were old ladies, and they kept us to a furious pace. One afternoon, as I flagged from heat and blisters, a grandmother, stooped beneath the weight of an enormous knapsack, overtook me wearing what appeared to be a pair of bedroom slippers.

We walked and prayed and then walked and prayed again. Only when darkness covered us did we lie down in our ponchos for a few hours of sleep, moving on again as soon as the first streaks of light appeared in the sky.

On the last morning, a gentle drizzle was falling when I awoke. Damp and cold, I peeked out of my poncho. In that first misty view of the day, I saw a woman kneeling on the wet grass just beyond me. Like most of the female pilgrims, who carried a minimum of supplies, she was wearing a lightweight plastic cape to protect herself from the rain. For a brief moment, I half believed that I was witnessing an apparition until the barely audible sound of her prayers reached my ears. I picked up a camera that I had been cradling all night just in time to take a picture before she stood up and walked over to her companions. Then I hurriedly rolled up my poncho to join them.

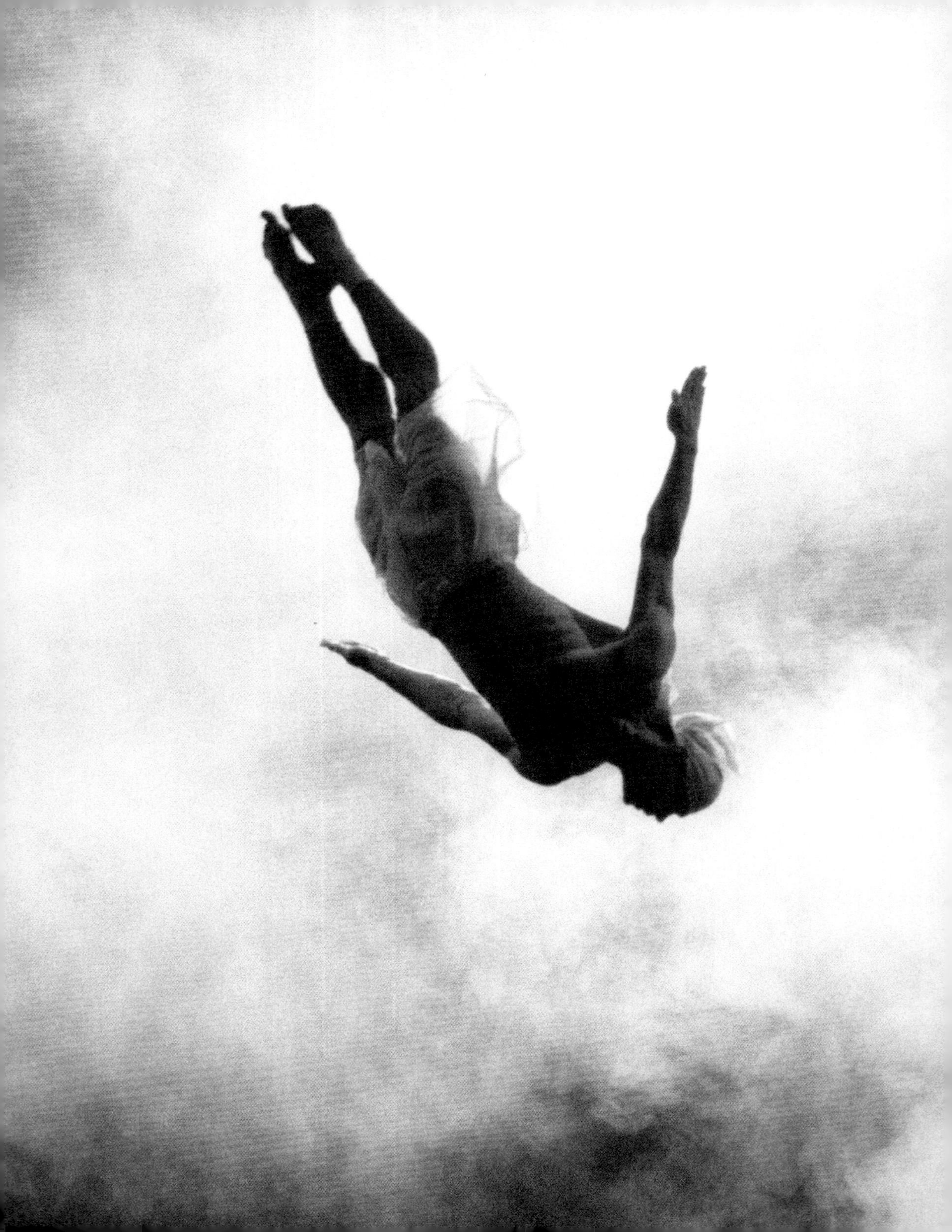

The Old Circus

Moscow
November 1997

Every self-respecting city in Russia has a circus, and I have often wondered whether the Soviet authorities once believed that these circular cathedrals could somehow replace the religious ones they were busy tearing down. Attending the circus, too, became a ritual, its iconography ingrained in the consciousness of Russians through movies and popular songs as well as through those visits on wintry days when Soviet children abandoned the cold reality in the streets for the man-made make-believe inside.

But in the 1990s the Russian circus, like almost every other institution in Russia, plunged into crisis. Many of the best artists headed to the West for better-paid work. Once thriving circuses struggled to buy food for their big animals—the local evening news in Russia during this period was filled with sad stories about starving elephants and tigers—and the talent pool that had streamed into the circus schools ran dry. Attending a performance was like watching a once proud and beautiful woman, thick make-up now covering the lines, clinging to past glories with the pretence that nothing had changed.

Part of the richness of the Russian circus is its reflection of the national character: by turns extravagant and outrageous, brilliant and atrocious, wavering precariously between the comic and the tragic. For all of these reasons, I became curious about the circus.

The Old Circus in Moscow, Russia's most famous, is not far from *The New York Times* office. A meeting with its legendary director, the clown Yuri Nikulin, furnished me with a press pass for the season, and I would often drop by to see part of the show. One night, I arrived just as a group of acrobats walked out to perform on the trampoline.

They were bare-chested and wore white bandanas and Lycra shorts adorned with pieces of chiffon, which, in combination with their hirsute torsos, seemed an uncertain feminine touch. As they started their act, a drummer beat out a rhythm and they jumped either singly or in pairs. Those acrobats not performing banged their fists on their chests in time with every leap. The jumps soared to increasingly dizzying heights as the act progressed and, in a kitschy effect, a fog-like smoke swamped the ring, silhouetting the performers. When the acrobats reached the top of their parabola, arching their bodies for the descent, they appeared to hover for an instant and the crowd inhaled as one, as if willing gravity's defeat.

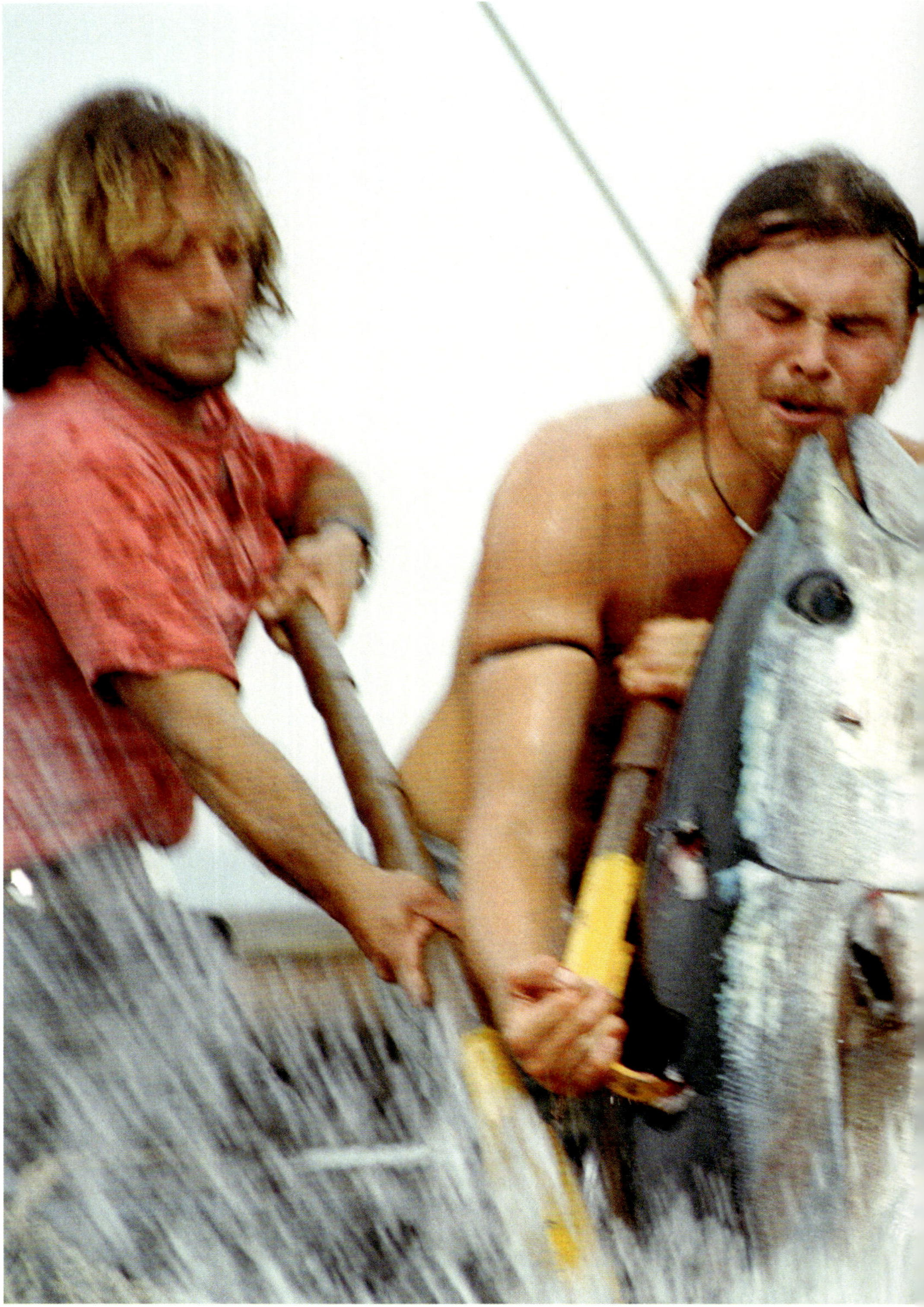

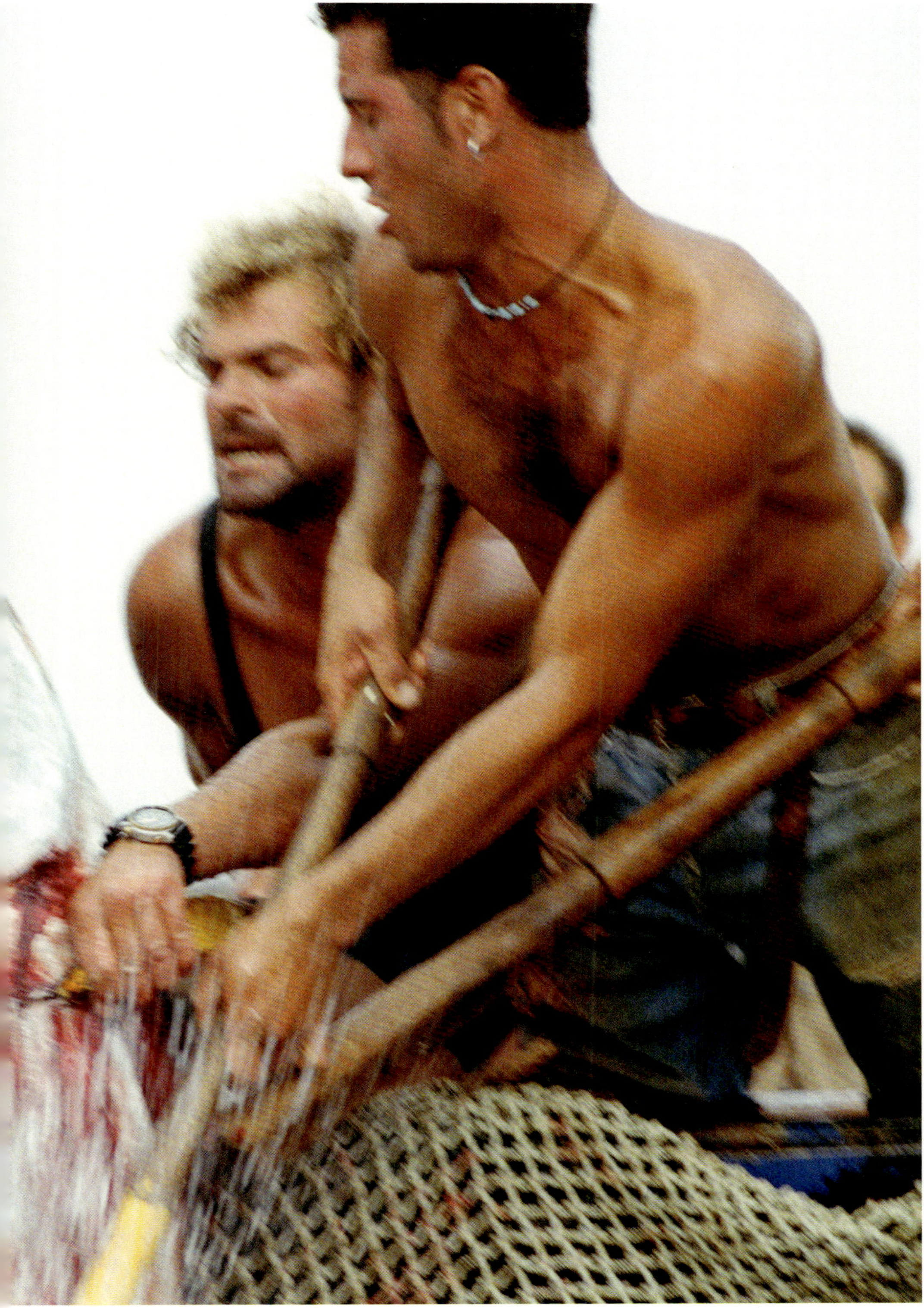

The Sicilian tuna harvest takes place in the cool aquamarine waters off the island of Favignana. I had rented a room in the house of Giovanni, a former fisherman, and his wife, Giovanna, for the princely sum of thirty thousand lira per night in order to see it.

The *mattanza,* meaning the "killing" (the word is derived from the Spanish *matar,* as in matador), is the island's traditional, highly ritualized, and not very efficient way of catching bluefin tuna by corralling them in a maze of nets as they return to their breeding grounds. A hundred and fifty years ago, when the sea was filled with fish, the deficiencies of this method were irrelevant. The tuna fishermen—the *tonnarotti*—were overwhelmed by the abundance of fish and caught up to ten thousand bluefin per season. By the 1990s, however, as sophisticated purse-seine fishing in the Mediterranean and factory trawlers in the Atlantic snared everything before them, the Sicilian fishermen were lucky to catch more than five hundred.

I flew in from Rome on a Friday. On Saturday, I awoke at 5:30 a.m. and walked down to the port to find the man known as the *rais,* the leader of the *tonnarotti.* The *rais,* whose title is a relic of Arab control of the islands, was an enormous man, bearded and tanned, who more closely resembled a pirate than a fisherman. He stared out across the bay, exuding the authority that such a title no doubt demanded, and in a stentorian voice ordered the fishermen to sea.

The *tonnarotti* set out in seven boats: six smaller boats, intended to hold three sides of the nets, and a larger one, to finish the square. But something was wrong. Although the sea was calm, when the men tried to pull

Mattanza

Favignana
10 June 1999

up the thick, heavy nets the current was too strong. After the *rais* and his men had spent five hours baking under the sun, they finally admitted defeat and headed home.

The next day was Sunday, so the fishermen rested. On Monday, they met at dawn in the bar by the port, which doubled as the *rais'* office. A heated conversation developed between the fishermen and the *rais*, and eventually everyone stepped outside to look at the sea. The noise abated as the *rais* scanned the horizon once more and pronounced that the current and the wind were still too strong. The *mattanza* would be postponed until the next day.

There is not much to do on Favignana. There are a few bars and restaurants, and a prison. I walked to the beach on the other side of the island to lie in the sun and forget that this assignment—as is so often the case when depending on animals—was not going according to plan. In the late afternoon, I returned to the house and told Giovanni that the *mattanza* had been postponed once again. He smiled at me sagely. "Tomorrow they will do it," he said, his voice hoarse from years of smoking and of shouting on the sea. "I am sure."

On Tuesday and Wednesday, there was still no *mattanza*. Each afternoon, I returned to the house, and each afternoon Giovanni would tell me the same thing. Finally, on Thursday, the conditions appeared to be perfect.

We embarked on a sea as flat as a millpond, the fishermen silent and nervous after having waited so long for the *mattanza* to begin. It took half an hour to reach the nets and for the boats to form the square over the final one, known as "the chamber of death." Slowly, methodically, the fishermen hauled up their catch, hand over hand, keeping time by singing traditional songs. They stopped when the nets were almost flat on the surface, dipping under the weight of the enormous tuna. The fish thrashed crazily in the water that remained, as if they understood that these were their final moments. Then the bloodbath began.

Several bare-chested fishermen descended from the main boat onto the nets, which hung between the boats like a circus net beneath a trapeze artist. Their dark bodies contrasted with the silver bellies of their prey, whose skin, smooth and sleek, flashed in the sunlight. The fishermen pushed the writhing tuna towards the main boat, where *tonnarotti* with long hooks pulled them close enough to be gaffed and hauled over the side. It took five or six men to heave one fish onto the boat—many of them weighed more than a hundred kilograms—and their hooks opened deep cuts in the tuna's flesh, sending blood cascading into the water below. In all, thirty-eight fish were pulled from the nets, turning the sea crimson.

When calm finally descended once more, the fishermen untied their boats from the nets and headed back to Favignana, leaving the blue of the sea to return. I remained on the larger boat as it sailed east to the port of Trapani, on the Sicilian coast; there a team of Japanese fishmongers eagerly awaited, to prepare the tuna for the sushi bars of Tokyo.

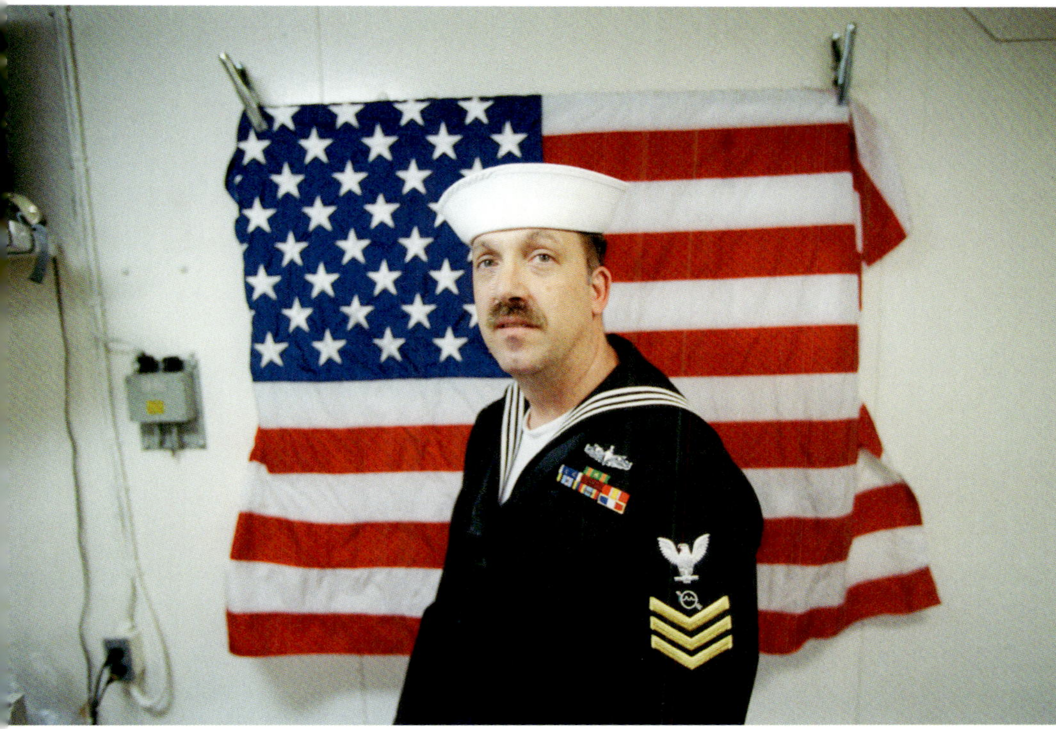

The Patriot

The U.S.S. Gonzalez, Somewhere in the Adriatic Sea
5 April 1999

Shortly after NATO began its bombing campaign against the Milošević regime during the Kosovo war, I flew on a Blackhawk helicopter from the Italian port of Bari to the U.S.S. Gonzalez, an American destroyer in the Adriatic that was launching Tomahawk missiles into Serbia.

Despite the destroyer's mission, I had the feeling of being on a cruise. The sea was calm and bright, and the destroyer turned ever so slowly, circling the Adriatic to maintain a particular distance from Belgrade. Officers took shifts peering through an enormous set of binoculars, as if the enemy might attack at any moment, and yet the horizon was always empty.

War came by night, when the Tomahawk missiles would roar out of their silos in a shroud of blinding light—making them almost impossible to photograph—before blazing away towards Serbia. Seconds later, the silence of the night would return, as if nothing had happened.

This push-button war confused me. Not that I yearned for the proximity of the front; I simply missed the reassurance of seeing who was fighting whom. Instead, I had only the heavens above and the sea below. The enemy existed merely as a dot on an electronic map.

The helicopter crew had promised to collect me after forty-eight hours but that deadline came and passed, and I was marooned. During the day, there was nothing to do. The ship sailed on and I wandered its corridors, unsure of what I was searching for.

One afternoon, I walked past a makeshift studio where the crew's photographer was taking portraits for the ship's log. A middle-aged, mustached sailor was posing in front of the Stars and Stripes. His presence immediately reassured me, if only because he was reminiscent of another, grittier era when ships fired guns rather than missiles, and an enemy was visible. His hat seemed to be perched so delicately on his head that a gust of wind would blow it off should he step out on deck, and its fragility, for no rational reason, made the ship real again to me.

By the time the Blackhawk returned, a week later, I had long lost any urge to rise for the nightly alarms of Tomahawk launches. Instead, I had come to crave the Southern fried chicken served daily by the ship's cook, who was homesick for Louisiana. As the helicopter took off and we rose above the Mediterranean, I could see the ship turning ever so slightly to starboard, beginning another circle.

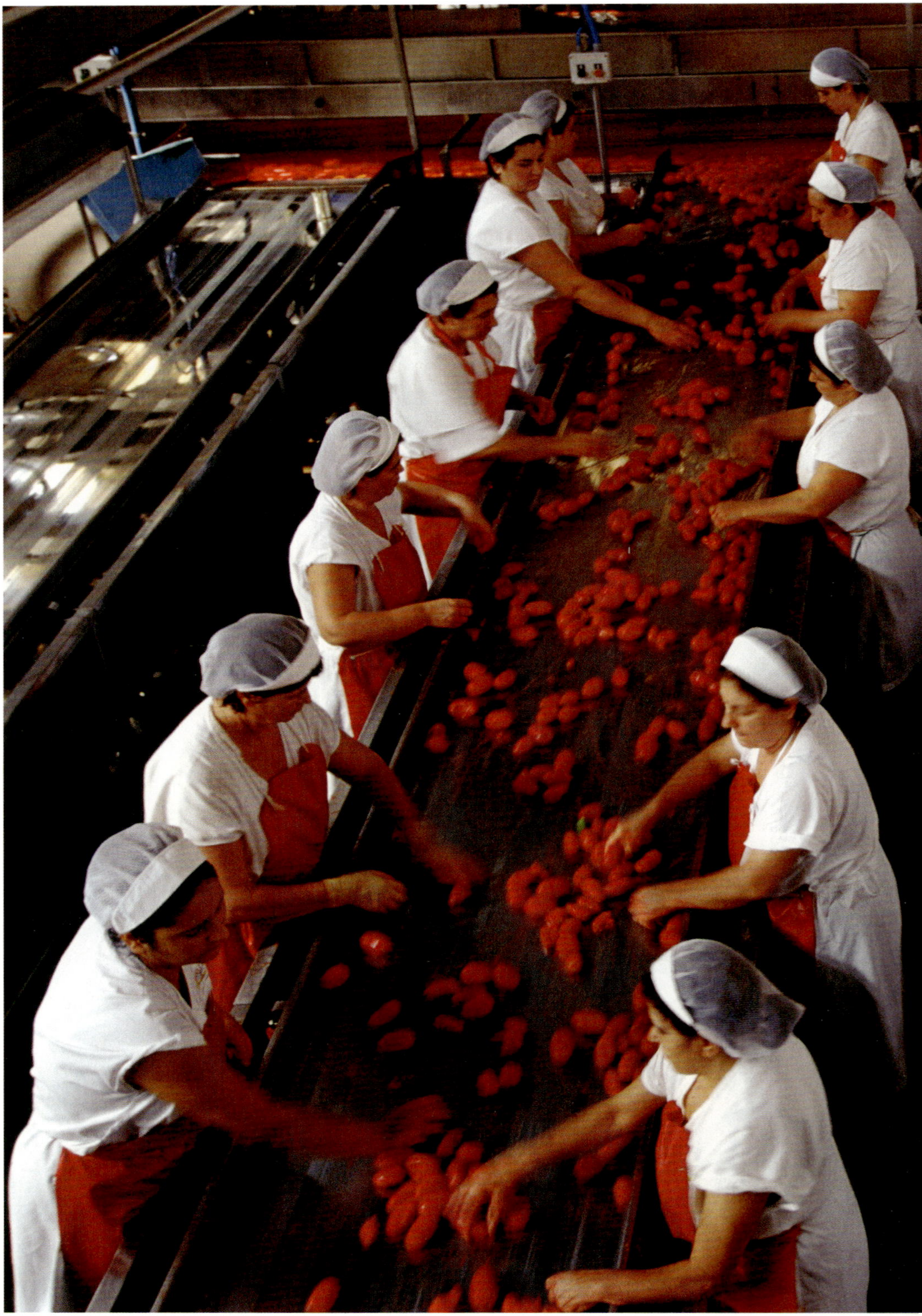

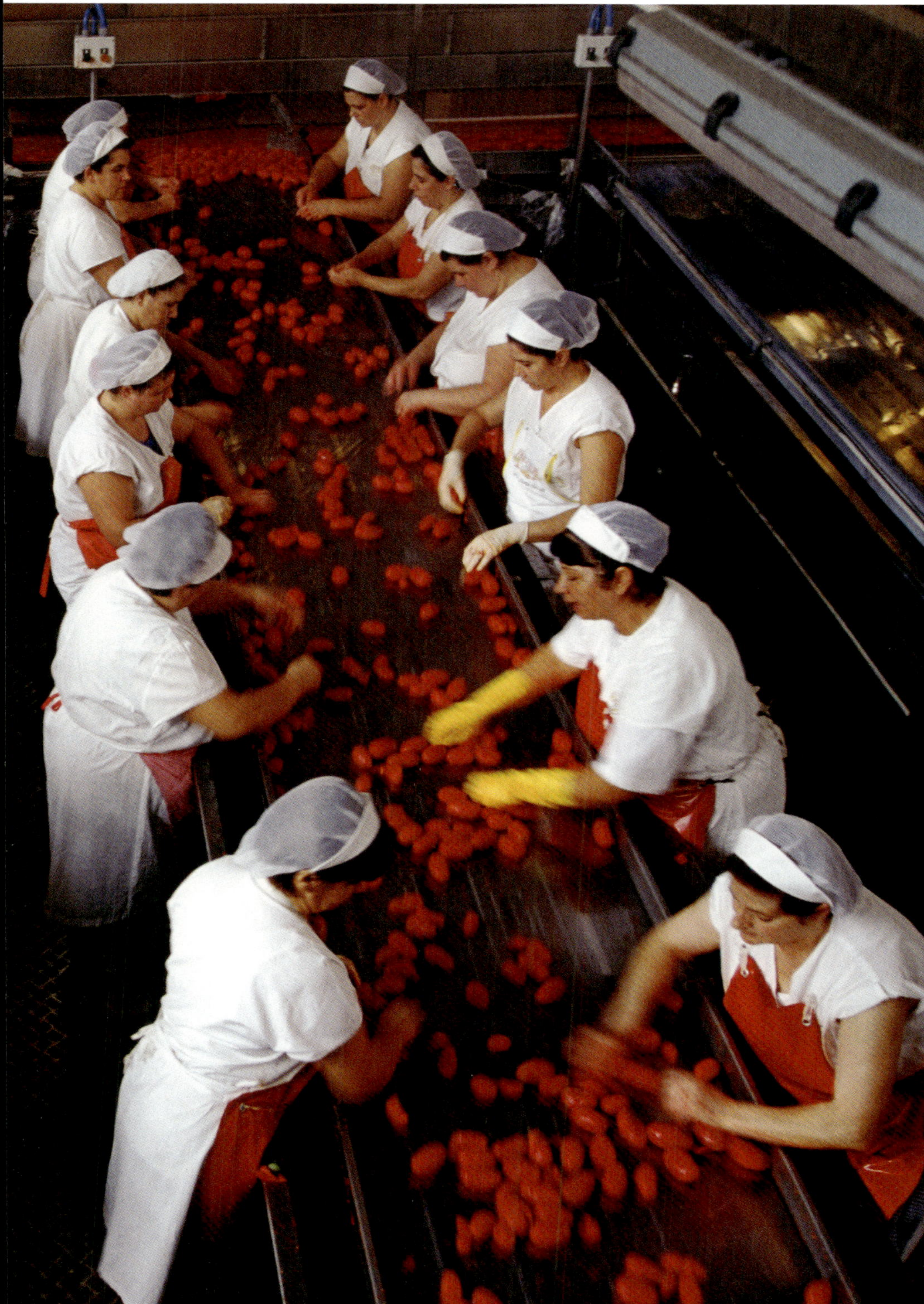

When I moved to Italy, in 1998, I entirely underestimated the country's obsession with food. Perhaps too many years of British and Slavic cooking had blunted my taste buds, but I found it difficult to imagine how a nation could hold a tomato in such high esteem. The tomato in question was a San Marzano—a plum-shaped tomato from the sun-kissed, ash-rich slopes beyond Mount Vesuvius. Admittedly, this tomato had a firm texture and a taste exquisitely balanced between sweetness and acidity that could send a self-respecting Italian matron into raptures about making *sugo*, the classic tomato sauce for pasta. But even so.

I have never been enthusiastic about photographing food, and the idea of photographing tomatoes was no exception. But I had no choice: the pictures were needed to accompany a story by the legendary *New York Times* writer Johnny Apple.

If I was to embark on an assignment that I didn't want, I decided that I needed, at least, a modicum of style. So I rented a soft-top car—albeit a far-from-new Fiat Punto—and left Rome on a brilliantly sunny morning for the road south to the village of San Marzano sul Sarno.

Beyond Naples, I reached an appointed rendezvous with two officials from the regional government. They

Stars in a Can

San Marzano, Italy
4 September 1999

sported thickly striped suits that looked as though they might have been bought at a sale of confiscated Mafia goods. I followed them to the village. We arrived at a tiny plot of land where a farmer stood waiting, holding a bunch of perfect red tomatoes—the last fruit of the harvest. This, apparently, was the highlight of the tour.

The councilmen and the farmer beamed at me, but I was far from happy with my photographs. We then went to a local restaurant for lunch, during which the president of the village co-operative made a speech and presented me with a crate holding twenty-five kilograms of tomatoes. Looking at the faces of the people seated next to me, I understood that resistance was useless. Smiling back, I thanked him profusely.

After lunch, the president told me that the director of the nearby Annalisa canning plant would show me his factory. Unfortunately, experience has invariably taught me that official tours rarely improve after lunch. But I resigned myself to his custody and followed his car to an industrial site fifteen kilometres away.

As we pulled up, my heart sank even further at the sight of the plant's bland, metallic exterior. Then he led me inside. Standing beside a series of conveyor belts were two dozen women in white coats, sorting tomatoes. It was as if Fellini himself had been expecting me and ordered up a cast of Italian mothers for my visit. I worked furiously, afraid that the women might suddenly disappear, and half an hour later—the women still sorting away—I was finished. The director then walked me back to the car and presented me with a case of twenty-four cans of San Marzano tomatoes.

It was early evening by the time I got back to Rome. As the light faded, I visited every bar and café I knew, begging people to take a few tomatoes. It wasn't easy. Perhaps there was something innately suspicious about an Englishman trying to give away tomatoes in Italy. When just a few remained, I allowed myself to return home, promising myself that I would make a *sugo*. For the next week, I stared at those tomatoes growing riper every day until they creased and formed black spots, and I had to throw them out.

A few days after the story was published, a card company in California wrote to me asking for the rights to print a thousand postcards of the picture. I have still not made *sugo* with San Marzano tomatoes, but one of those cards sits proudly on the shelf in my kitchen.

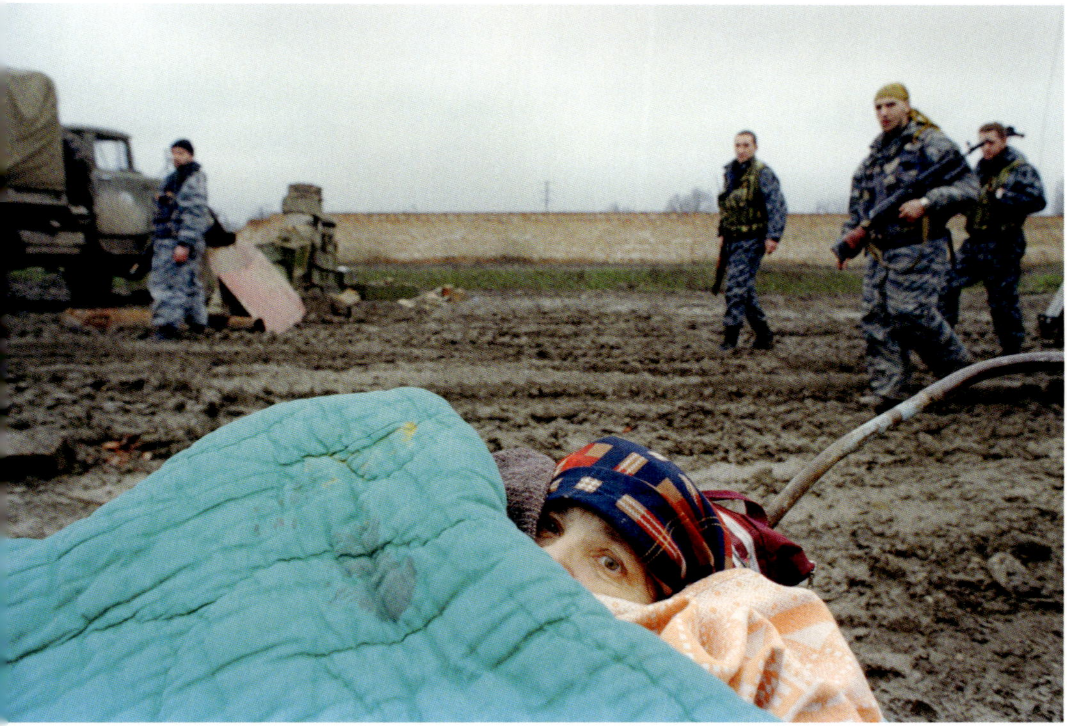

During the first Chechen war, in 1994–96, most journalists led a charmed life, able to cross the front lines at will, largely respected by both sides and untroubled by the kidnapping that was to scourge Chechnya in the conflict's aftermath. But by the time Russian forces re-invaded Chechnya, in 1999, unhindered movement for the press had become virtually impossible. The Chechen forces had splintered into wildly disparate groups with shifting allegiances and a general hostility to outsiders, including journalists. The Russians, for their part, made no secret of their mistrust of the foreign press, believing that many reporters romanticised the Chechen cause, and that their access to the front should be minimal. Only when the Russian advance towards Grozny, the Chechen capital, gathered momentum and victory over the rebels was in sight did the Russians allow us near the fighting and even then we were under tight supervision.

Our rendezvous was at a miserable garrison town, Mozdok, in the republic of North Ossetia, neighbouring Chechnya. Since Ossetia was Christian, the Russians felt safe there. But the moment we crossed the border into Chechnya itself the troops guarding us became nervous, pulling masks over their faces and wedging our smoky old bus between two armoured personnel carriers for protection. On a later tour I made the mistake of having four cups of tea for

The Grandmother

Staraya Sunzha, Chechnya
15 January 2000

breakfast; during a brief stop, deep inside Chechnya, I was still urinating when the soldiers reboarded, and they threatened to shoot me for endangering the convoy.

The war was also different because of the new Russian Prime Minister, Vladimir Putin. After the disgrace of losing the first war, he wanted to eradicate the Chechen rebels—even if, as he famously stated, it meant blowing them up in their outhouses. The scale of the destruction was overwhelming, and as we passed one flattened house after another our minders from the Foreign Ministry grew increasingly silent.

Nearly four hours after our journey began, we reached the front at Staraya Sunzha, a suburb of Grozny; the battle for the Chechen capital raged barely half a kilometre down the road. We disembarked at a staging post where troops from Russian Interior Forces were gathering, checking their machine guns, and adjusting their bandanas à la Rambo. They scowled, raising their guns to indicate, presumably jokingly, that they would open fire if I took their picture.

More ordnance landed on Grozny during that campaign than on any other city in Russia since World War Two. Our guides from the Ministry, already deeply ill at ease with the booming explosions in the distance, were refusing to let me move farther down the road when a trickle of refugees—mostly poor, ethnic Russians—came trudging towards us.

I rushed to them, at first not noticing the old woman lying in a wheelbarrow. Her son, who had been struggling to push her, told me that she had been wounded by falling masonry on New Year's Day but that the bombardment of the city had been so unrelenting that they had been stranded in their shattered home. For ten days, he had tended to her wounds before seizing on a lull in the fighting to evacuate her in the only available transport, his wheelbarrow. Even then it had taken him five days to push her the fifteen kilometres to the outskirts of the city where we stood that afternoon.

Turning to the woman, I crouched next to her, taking pictures as she stared at me, her eyes unblinking. After a minute, her silence stopped me and I felt forced to speak to her, uttering words of comfort in Russian that I did not believe—and probably neither did she—yet which nonetheless seemed important to say. She did not reply. I was still talking to her when the minders from the Foreign Ministry, declaring the departure of the bus to be imminent, pulled me away, presumably horrified that another miserable story might present itself at any moment.

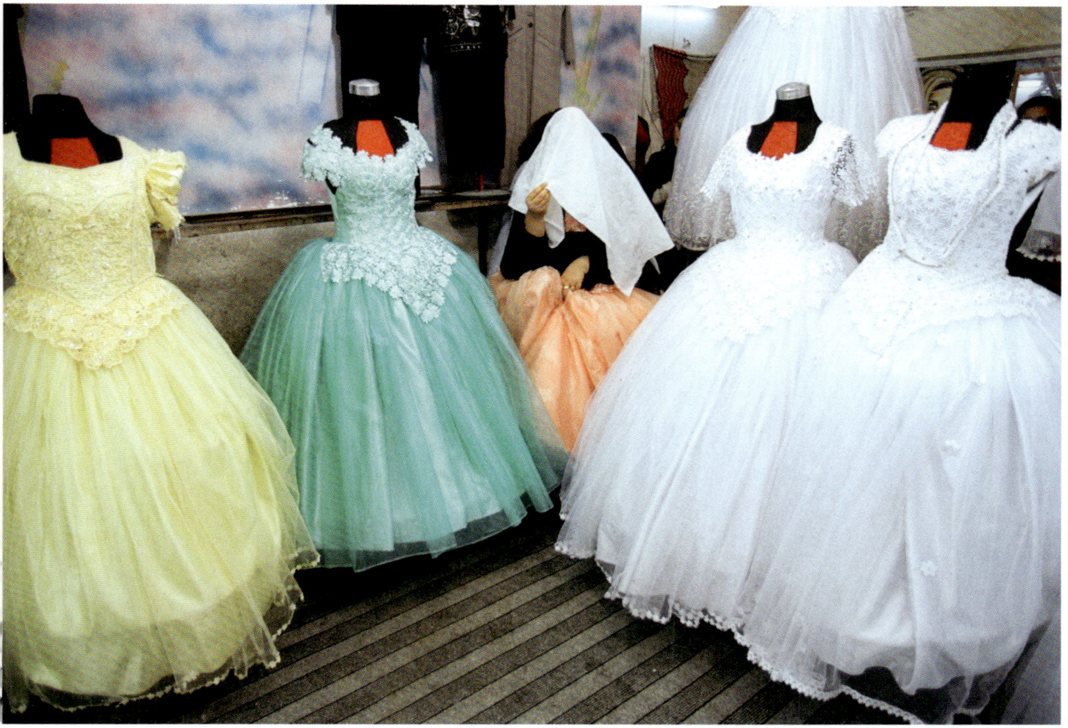

The journey to the macabre land of Saddam Hussein's Iraq began across the border, in Jordan, at a mock Babylonian palace the colour of lapis lazuli that was the Iraqi Embassy in Amman.

I rang the bell one morning and a thin, mustachioed official clasping a cigarette opened the door, ushering me to a dusty sofa in a room whose sole decoration was a portrait of Saddam Hussein. After waiting ten minutes, I was invited into an inner sanctum where another mustachioed man sat at a desk. He offered me tea and a visa-application form, and said that I should call in a few days to see if the visa was ready.

I duly telephoned two days later, but no one answered. So that morning and the following ones I walked down to the embassy to ask if approval for the visa had come through. I would drink tea or coffee with the same mustachioed consul, after which he would make a call—real or not, I couldn't tell—and tell me to come back the next day.

Finally, after a week and several hundred dollars in additional consular fees, I received the visa. The consul congratulated me on the successful outcome and suggested that his cousin might drive me overnight to Baghdad to avoid any problems at the border.

It was a cold and overcast night, and the lights of Amman soon faded into the desert as the consul's cousin navigated our way to the Iraqi border and then through a myriad of officials with bushy moustaches. Within half an hour, we were tearing down a vast and ghostly German-built motorway towards Baghdad.

The Wedding Shop

Saddam City, Baghdad
14 March 2001

When we arrived in the Iraqi capital, at dawn, each street revealed a different guise of the country's leader: Saddam the general, Saddam the sheikh, Saddam the world leader in a Western suit, Saddam in a cardigan and a Tyrolean hat—the symbolism of which entirely escaped me. He was everywhere and nowhere, omnipresent yet invisible.

It was still a surprise to arrive at the Al-Rasheed Hotel in central Baghdad and see, on the floor in front of the entrance, the mosaic caricature of former President George Bush, along with the words "Bush Is Criminal." The doormen watched closely to make sure that I didn't sidestep his face; I trod on his hair rather than on his mouth, just to irritate them.

The man at reception automatically assigned me a room facing the Indian Ocean—it was possible to connect to the outside world only by satellite phone—and these rooms were doubtlessly bugged. Even so, every time I opened my door onto the shag-carpeted corridor, I found a man in a brown suit and slippers shuffling past.

While working in Iraq I was essentially in the custody of the Ministry of Information at all times. I could go out for a meal, but I was unable visit anyone without my minder. No spontaneous response to anything was possible, because I could not take a single photograph without direct permission. Like most foreign journalists, I was led around a well-trodden circuit, starting with a visit to a hospital with undernourished babies. While I didn't doubt that some of the children I saw were suffering indirectly because of international sanctions, this explanation was so overplayed that it was difficult to make sense of what I was being shown.

During the next weeks, I was taken to visit markets and schools in Baghdad, the date fields of Basra, the Marsh Arabs of the Shatt al-Arab, and the gaudy recreation of ancient Babylon, a disjointed vision of the country specifically designed to camouflage any glimpses of reality.

On the last day, we stopped in Saddam City, the Shiite ghetto of Baghdad. The Ministry of Information wished to squash any rumours about Saddam Hussein's repression of the Shiite community. We weaved through the bustling district until my guide, puffing furiously on his cigarette, got out of the car and led me into a wedding parlour.

The moment we stepped in, all the women—several of whom were obviously preparing for weddings later that day—disappeared into the back, and I was left staring at a display of frocked mannequins. I stood, waiting, wondering what would happen next, when suddenly a bride rushed towards the door to the street, a towel clasped over her face. As I took her picture, I could not help but reflect on the paradox of this land of mirrors where, when I was permitted take a photograph, the person's identity remained completely hidden.

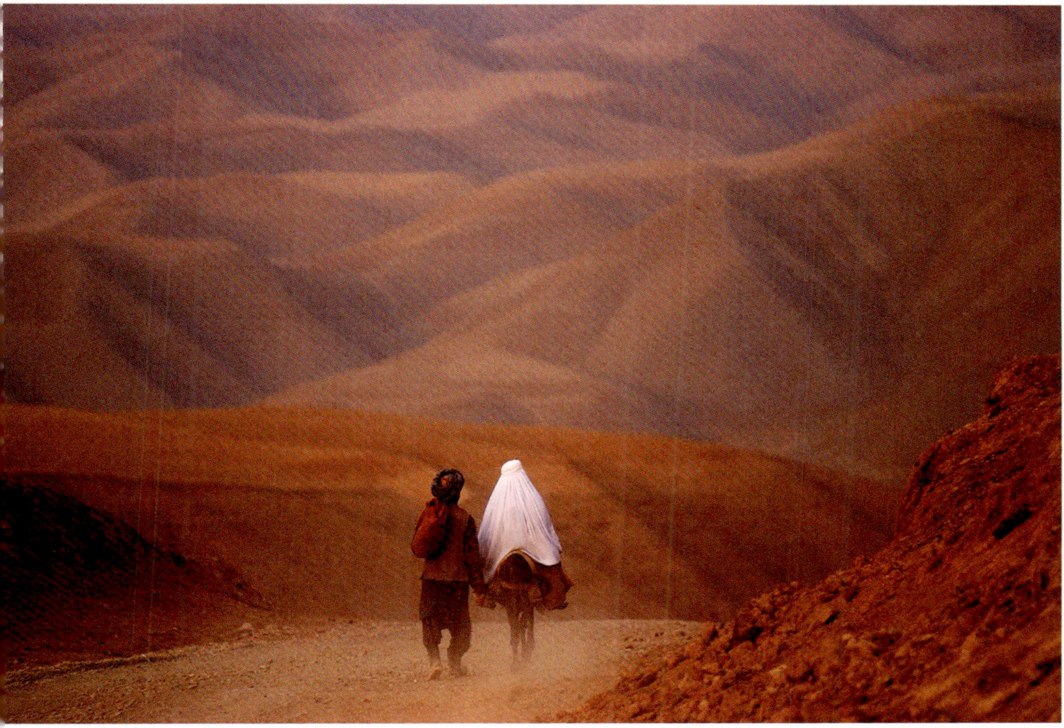

The Couple

Badakhshan Province, Afghanistan
19 October 2001

When I first saw the lone couple silhouetted against the barren mountains, I hesitated. They seemed like a mirage that would disappear as soon I approached, a concern that was reinforced by my overwhelming desire to take their picture.

I was still recovering from a bewildering day spent with one of the local Northern Alliance commanders, who had greeted me early that morning on the top of a magnificent range of mountains. With a nonchalant air, mapping out the terrain in front of us, he pointed to a distant peak where he said the Taliban were dug in. Then he ordered his two tanks to start shelling their positions. By some peculiar agreement, each side took turns shelling the other, and today was the Northern Alliance's go.

The tanks fired at random and a chorus of soldiers standing nearby shouted, "*Allahu Akbar*" with each departing shot. After two hours, the shelling abruptly stopped, as if the Alliance's allotted time for firing had expired, and the soldiers retired to a mud hut. I followed them—there was nothing else to do—and found them smoking a joint and carrying a cumbersome antenna around the room, attempting to pick up channels on their ancient television. After few minutes of trial and error, they stumbled upon a women's tennis tournament; the display of bare thighs and arms reduced them to silence and then, when one of the players grunted, sent them into fits of hysterics. Feeling superfluous to the scene, I returned to the jeep and began the slow descent to the valley.

Just after we reached the main road, I saw the couple ahead of us. Their tender proximity appeared so delicate that our very presence on that empty road seemed to threaten it. I took a few frames as they bisected the view and then put down my cameras and listened instead to the clickety-clack of the donkey's hooves piercing the stillness of the dusk.

I felt mysteriously recalibrated by the couple's slow, sure progress. After we drove past, I continued to follow them in the side mirror until they vanished.

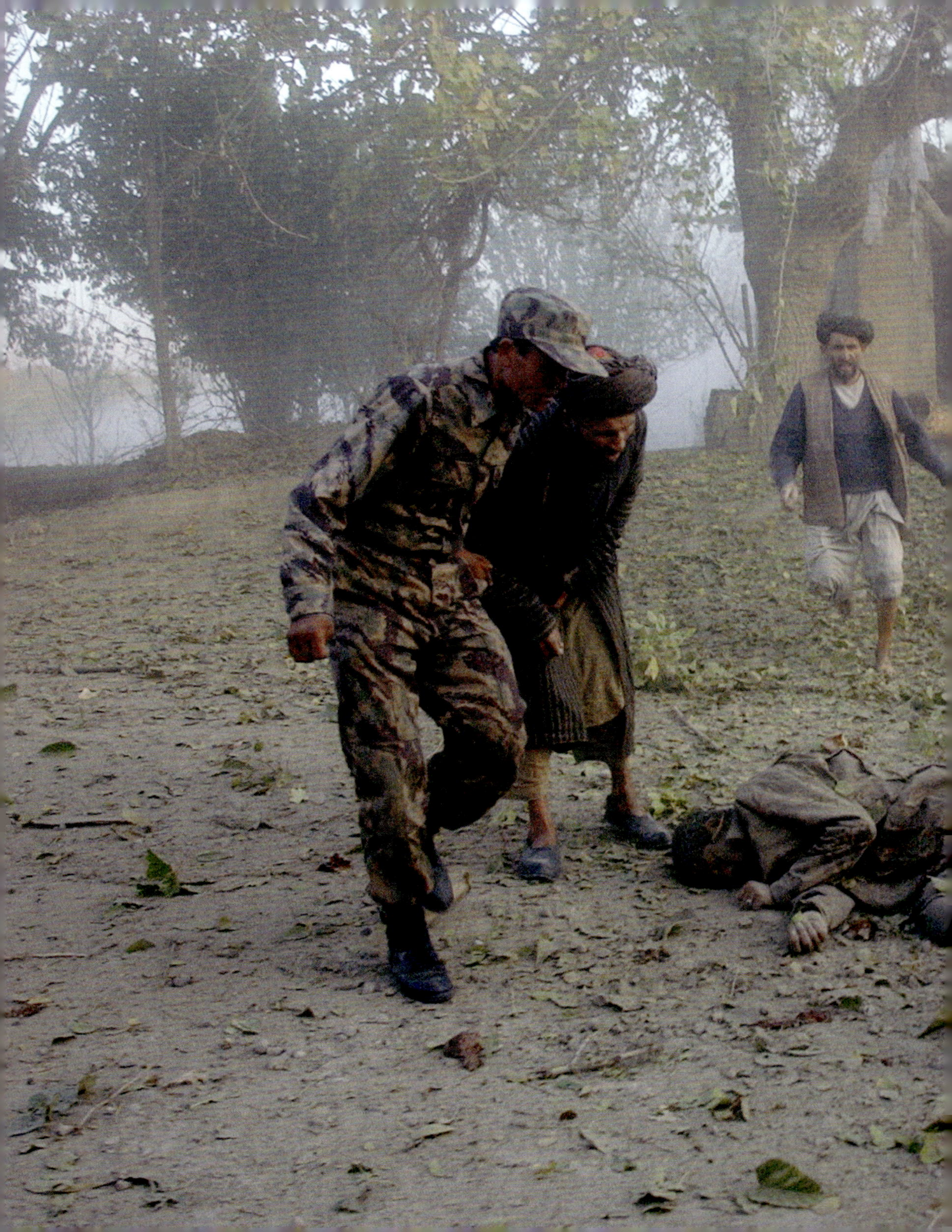

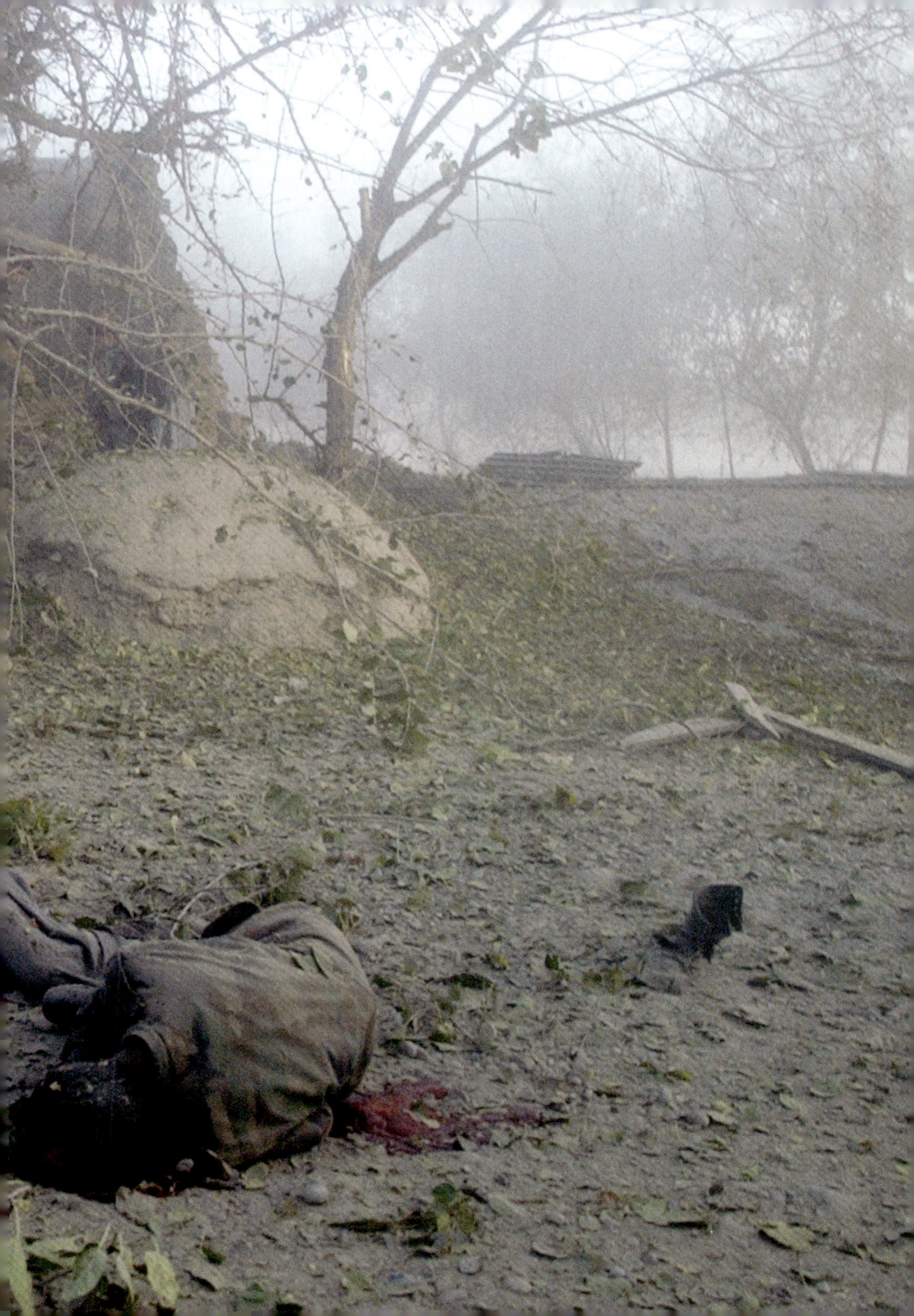

I was sent to Afghanistan by *The New York Times* in the autumn of 2001 to cover the Northern Alliance's offensive against the Taliban. It was an important assignment for me; there were only two photographers in the country for the paper, and we had each been given a different region. Every time I went to the front, however, the Alliance's soldiers seemed far too busy sipping cups of tea to fight.

The rest of the time, I was whiling away my days in the dusty hamlet of Khwaja Bohaouddin, the stronghold of the Northern Alliance, where my quarters consisted of a mud house and a yard. Despite the fact that everyone discussed the advance feverishly, after a month I began to fear that it would never take place.

By November, I was beside myself with frustration and impatience. When news came one day that a local warlord, to celebrate his daughter's marriage, was organising a game of bushkazhi—a wild, Afghan version of polo, played with a dead goat rather than with sticks—I was delighted to have the chance to attend. It was only late that afternoon, as Dexter Filkins, my colleague from *The New York Times*, and I were driving home with our translators, that I glimpsed the distant pattern of contrails over the frontline and realised I was missing the war I'd been sent to photograph.

The Stray Shell

Dashti Qala, Afghanistan
10 November 2001

We implored our driver to take us as fast as possible towards the front, close to the neighbouring village of Dashti Qala, and he scarcely braked, throwing us first against one side of our Soviet-made UAZ jeep and then against the other as we hurtled down the deserted road. That afternoon I believed utterly in my lucidity, even as we rushed towards what common sense urged me to avoid. I felt no fear—my fear in such moments was already long gone—only a heightened sense of anticipation, as if waiting with complete certainty for something dramatic to happen.

Still, it was an unbelievable shock when a shell landed on the road only fifty metres in front of our jeep, sending a huge sheet of fire up into the sky. A second later, the sound wave from the explosion threw us violently backwards in our seats. The driver instinctively braked to a standstill, but I screamed at him to continue towards the vast ball of smoke rising just ahead.

When we lurched to a stop once more, just short of where the shell had landed, and I jumped out of the car, everyone and everything was suddenly very quiet and still. Three soldiers had been hit and were either dead or dying—two of them lying in the road, and the other in a ditch to the side. The one in the ditch moved an arm slowly as his life ebbed away. Even as I photographed his companions, I anaesthetised myself to what I was seeing, refusing to accept its reality.

By the time I went to Afghanistan, I was familiar with the spectacle of watching mankind stepping over the edge, and each time I wanted to peer a little further. Yet my ability to distinguish between the real and the surreal was becoming increasingly compromised. Taking the image was instinctive, automatic; only much later, after I returned home, would the final traces of numbness lift, and I would then feel the pain of what I had seen. It was as if each image of violence I took left a small shard of glass inside me, a wound that could never entirely heal. And yet the next time I was asked to cover another war, I would pick up my bags and go.

Two civilians and an officer who had been spared rushed over to these soldiers as I took their pictures. I assumed that they would offer the men some sort of help or comfort, but there seemed to be no question of help—or of weeping, either. The officer merely shooed me away. I climbed back in the jeep, and we continued on to the front line. When we returned through the checkpoint, two hours later, the bodies had already been taken away for burial. Only a small crimson patch of sand remained.

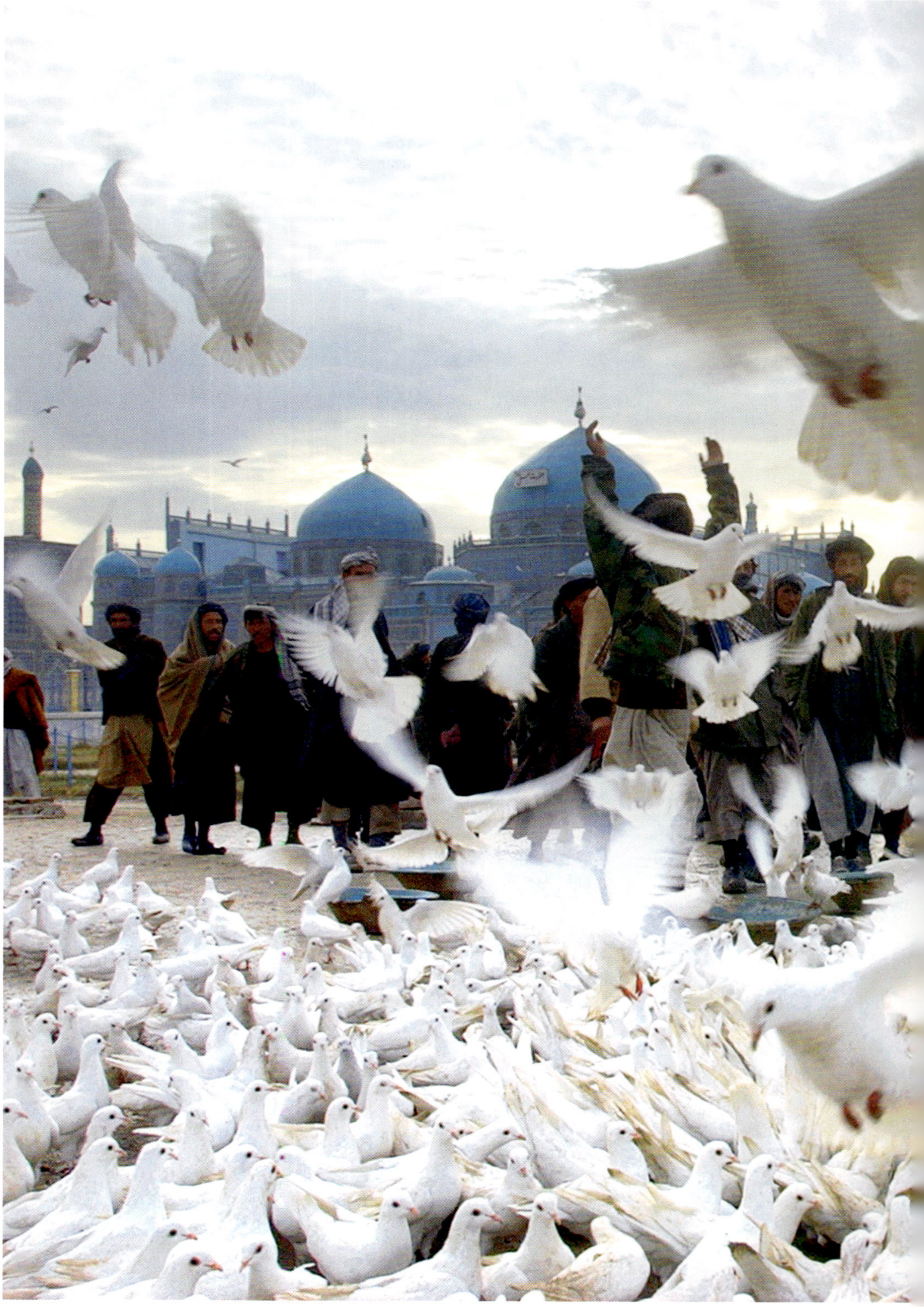

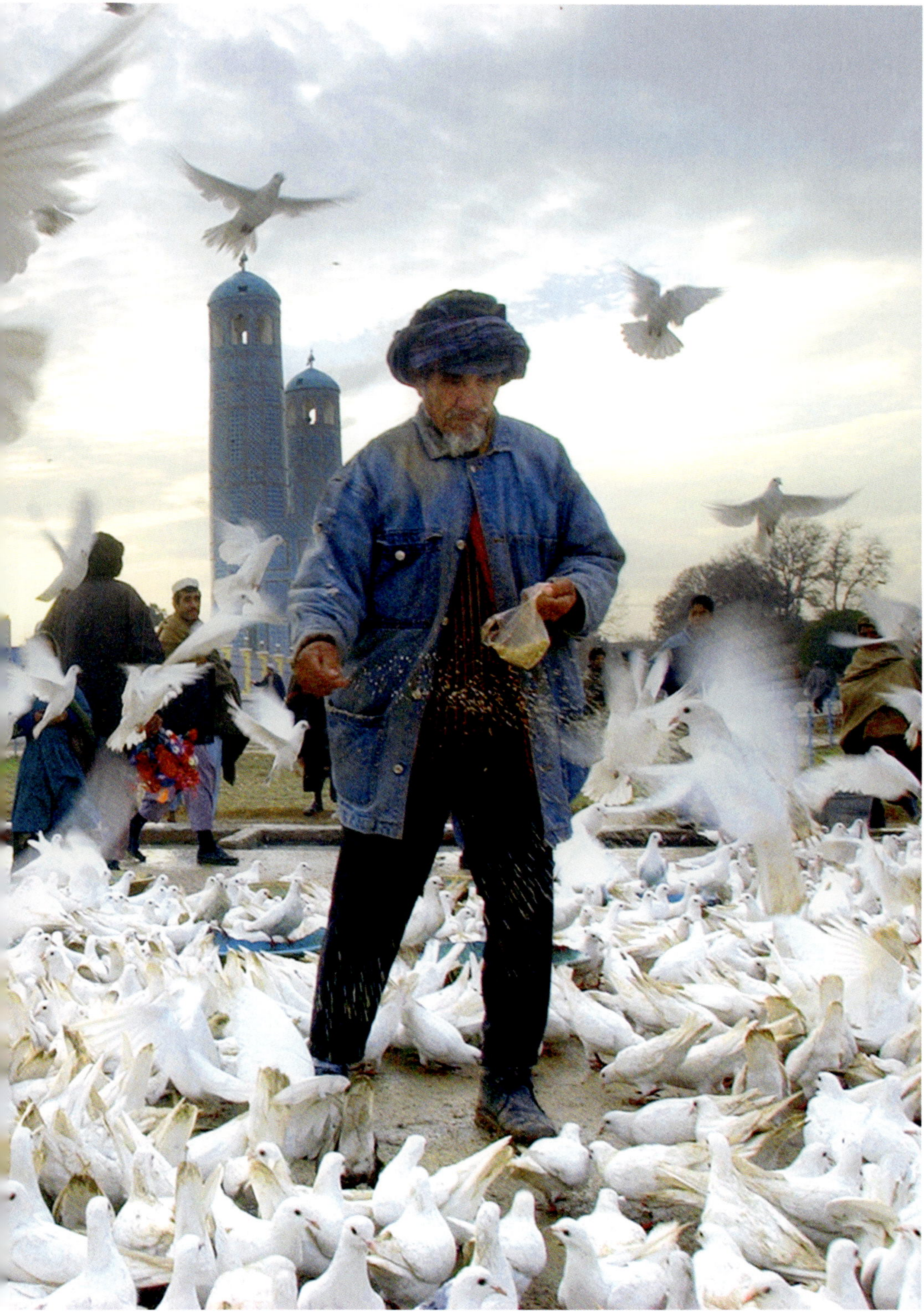

The Island of Peace

Hazrat Ali Mosque, Mazar-i-Sharif
30 November 2001

Each morning in Afghanistan, I would wake up thinking about my imminent journey down dusty dirt roads to the front line—a mountainous landscape invariably punctuated by men with Kalashnikovs whose stares told me nothing of their intentions.

My behavior became instinctive, like that of an animal trying to smell its way to safety, and when I arrived at the doors of the Red Cross residence in Mazar-i-Sharif after two months in the country I had become part savage. Sitting at dinner that first night, clad in a hastily cleaned shirt and trousers, I gazed at the place settings and candles with a sense of profound estrangement, recognising all the trappings of my culture but feeling entirely alien to it. Polite conversation, of any sort, was out of the question.

It was, perhaps, not a coincidence that Mazar-i-Sharif, the capital of northern Afghanistan, was offering a temporary return to my other world, since the city itself was a paradoxical place, beautified by turquoise minarets and yet haunted by a violent and vengeful history.

In 1997, at the height of the civil war, hundreds of Taliban were executed in the desert just outside the city's gates. When the Taliban returned in force the next year, they left a sign to mark their exploits. "By God's grace," the text by the eastern gate of the city stated, "the Taliban captured the northern region of Afghanistan in 1998 and massacred the pagans."

Mazar-i-Sharif seemed a city without room for mercy. Just as I arrived, Uzbek forces of the Northern Alliance, led by General Abdul Rashid Dostum and aided by American Special Forces, were suppressing an uprising of Taliban prisoners in the Qala-i-Jangi fortress, leaving a carpet of bodies on the prison's grounds.

So brutal was the battle's conclusion that a dramatic and awkward peace descended on the city; having visited the fortress to photograph the aftermath, I wandered aimlessly, in a state of confusion, as if searching for the answer to a question that I wasn't able to define. As I crisscrossed the city, my path invariably took me through the central square and past the Hazrat Ali mosque, Afghanistan's most sacred site.

The mosque is named after Ali, the son of the Prophet Muhammad and one of the pivotal figures of the Shia branch of Islam. Although Ali is buried in Najaf, in modern-day Iraq, according to local legend his spirit resides in Mazar-i-Sharif. Here a sentinel of hundreds of doves—supposedly descendants of a pair brought in the seventeenth century by an Afghan prince coming back from Najaf—stand watch over him.

Local residents said that a few days before, doves had suddenly begun returning to the mosque, offering them a sense of hope. And I, too, felt cheered in their presence. Visitors arrived to feed them—not only as a sign of religious devotion but also as thanks for the symbol of peace they represented in the sea of violence that had engulfed Afghanistan.

Many legends have sprung up around the birds, each one more astonishing than the next, and almost everyone I talked to offered a different story. One man attributed a spirit to every seventh dove; another claimed that if a grey pigeon landed amongst the crowd it would turn white within forty days to assimilate itself with its hallowed brethren. Because the doves decided to position themselves perfectly when I took this photograph, I was happy to believe every tale.

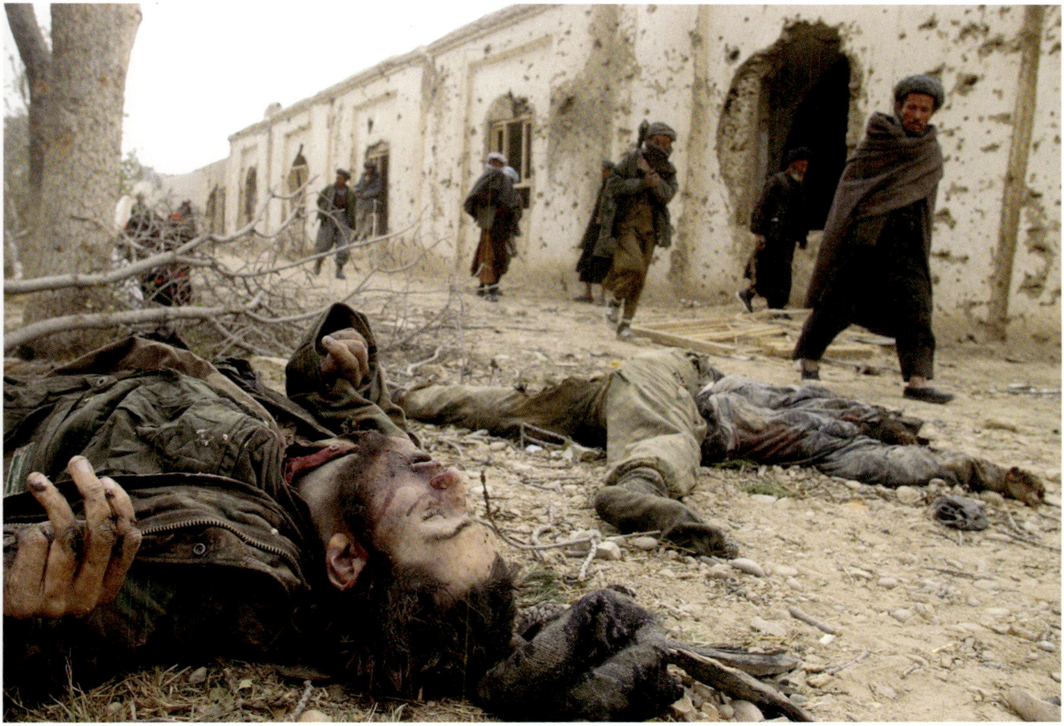

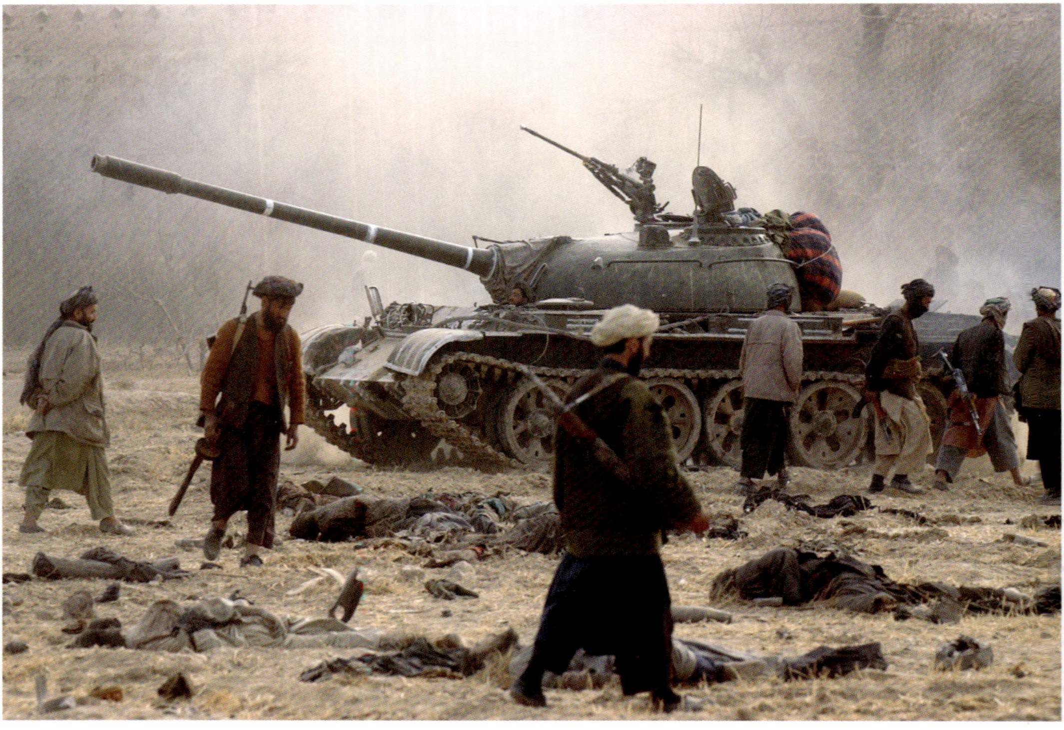

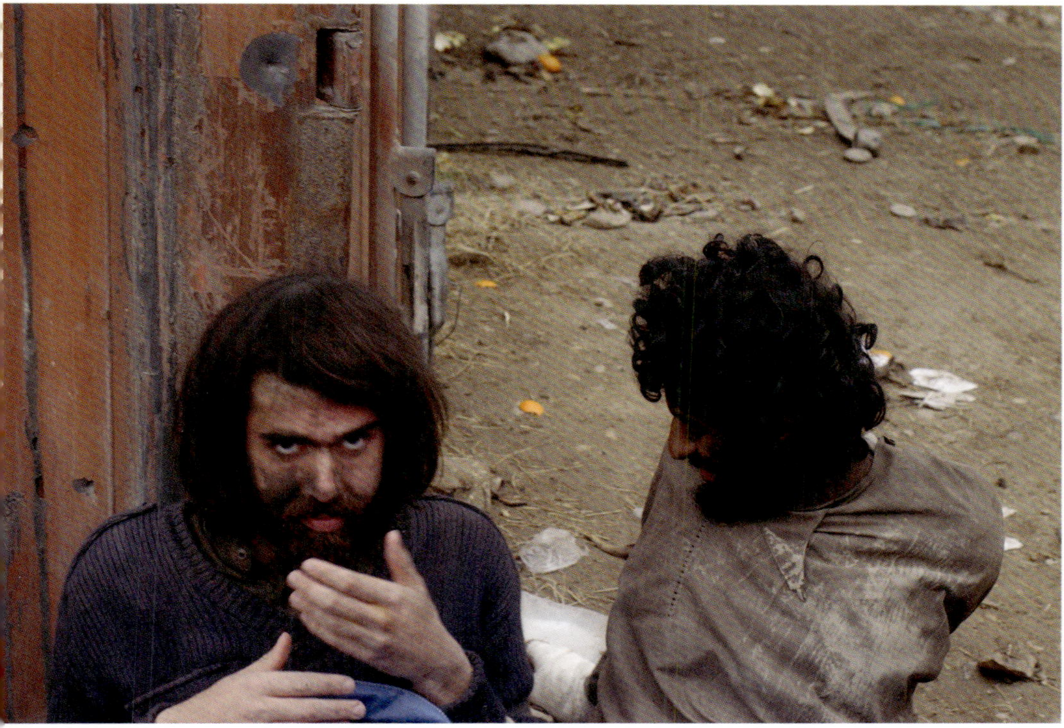

I took only two pictures of John Walker Lindh, the American Taliban: one when he had his eyes covered, and the other when he brought down his hands to see if I was still standing there. Then he asked me not to take any more pictures, and I stopped. I don't know why, but I did. Looking at his blackened face, I felt sorry for him, even though there was little reason to do so.

A guard had pointed him out to me a few minutes earlier, saying that he was from Inglistan. Lindh corrected him, saying that he was American. Because he spoke with an accent that seemed Pakistani or Indian, I did not believe him: he resembled a caveman more than a Californian. I found it strange, too, that someone would boast about being an American at that particular moment, unless he felt that he would be safer facing American justice—there were American Special Forces in town—rather than General Dostum's; the Uzbek commander's care had never proved particularly healthy for prisoners.

As I was editing my photographs that night, I almost deleted those two pictures. Space was running out on my computer and my spare hard drive, and the photographs of yet another prisoner did not seem to be important. On that grey afternoon, he was just one

American Taliban

Qala-i-Jangi Fortress, Mazar-i-Sharif
1 December 2001

more grimy, bearded Taliban foot soldier sitting on the ground at the Qala-i-Jangi fortress. But a few days later, when his identity became clear, I was enormously relieved to find his face among those images.

Unbeknownst to me, Johnny Spann, a C.I.A. agent, had spotted Lindh a week before. Lindh had claimed to be Irish, but before the agent could interrogate him further the Taliban prisoners had overpowered and killed their guards and Spann, sparking a bloody and brutal battle. U.S. Special Forces and jets and a host of Northern Alliance troops pounded the jail's compound during a three-day confrontation.

When I arrived at the fortress the morning after the fighting finally subsided, hundreds of bodies lay on the ground. So densely clustered were the casualties that I accidentally stepped on a corpse's hand, snapping some finger bones as I crouched to get a better angle. Like a good Englishman, I almost turned to apologise before catching myself.

For General Dostum and his troops, however, the carnage was underwhelming. I saw one soldier removing gold teeth from a corpse with a pair of pliers. Another soldier, driving a T-55 tank, squashed bodies left and right as he crisscrossed the prison grounds.

But as I walked through the fortress a few hours later, gunshots suddenly rang out. Northern Alliance soldiers had discovered a group of armed prisoners who had taken refuge in a bunker.

For several days I returned to watch Dostum's forces attempt to flush them out. First the troops fired grenade launchers. Then they poured fuel down the bunker steps and set it alight. When that failed, they flooded the bunker, at which point the prisoners, a burnt, miserable and bedraggled bunch, finally surfaced. That was when I saw Lindh for the first time.

Half an hour later, I found him again, sitting in the back of an open-top truck, with a bunch of bananas on his lap that had been given to him by a Red Cross worker. When I raised my camera, he turned his head away, whispering, "If you have already taken my picture, you should burn it." Again, I put my camera down. When he turned back to me and saw that I was no longer taking photographs, he spoke a few words about his ordeal, describing how he had watched prisoners drown and burn to death. Yet he spoke without emotion, as if he cared little for their fate and even less for his own—as if resigned to the fact that he had ceased to be an adventurer and had metamorphosed, instead, into a traitor.

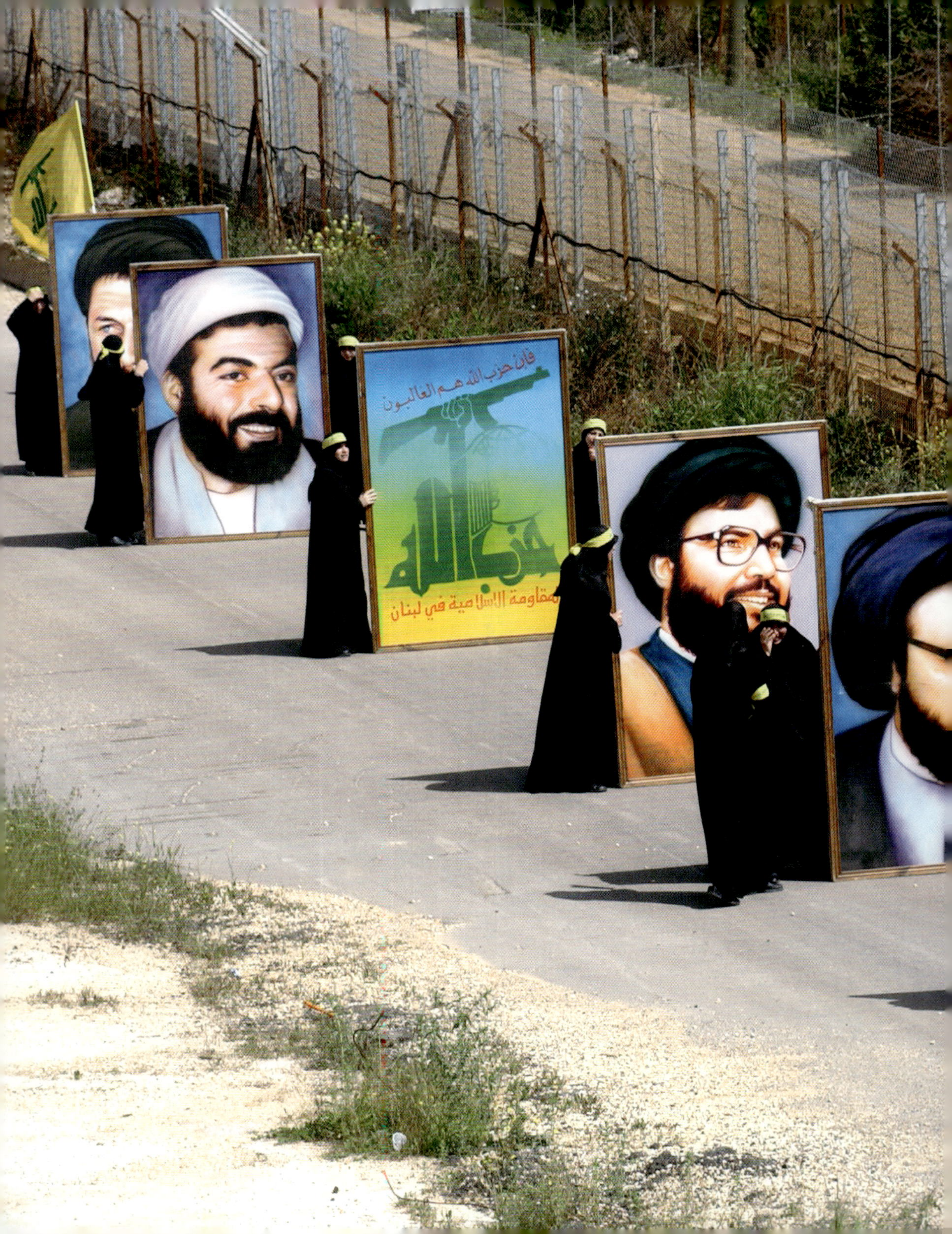
فإن حزب الله هم الغالبون
حزب الله
مقاومة الإسلامية في لبنان

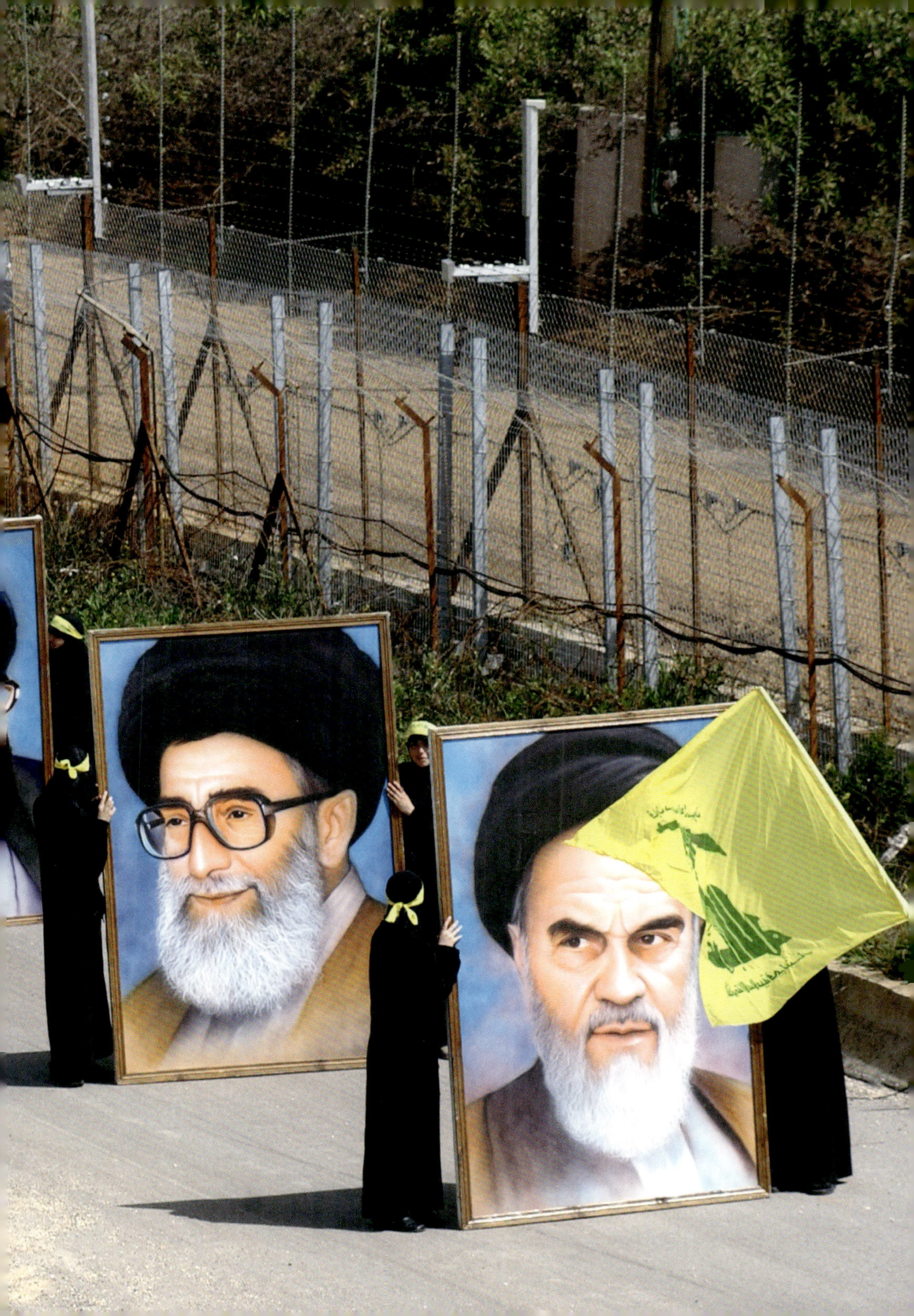

When one drives south from Beirut, the road turns away from the Mediterranean and winds through valleys dotted with olive trees until it arrives at a checkpoint on the banks of the Litani River. This is where government-controlled territory ends and the land of Hezbollah, the Party of God, begins. There is, of course, no official internal border in Lebanon. Nevertheless, Hezbollah has run this border zone from the day that the Israeli forces left Lebanon in 2000.

It is land that men have fought over for as long as anyone can remember. The enormous Crusader castle of Beaufort, standing high above the town of Nabatieh, has borne witness to the centuries of battles waged here. Even as late as the 1970s, the castle was a base—first for the P.L.O., and then for the Israelis, who dynamited large parts of the fortifications as they withdrew their troops.

Hezbollah's message is proclaimed at every turn of the road, on billboards showing grainy images of attacks on Israeli convoys and portraits of martyrs bearing AK-47 assault rifles. In the Middle East, where political dialogue has long been a shouting match, these images screamed at me. And, in case I was in danger of forgetting the ultimate goal, signposts every few kilometres marked the distance to Jerusalem. The Party of God has always been nothing if not relentless.

The Party of God

Fatima Gate, Lebanese-Israeli Border
14 April 2002

When I photographed their leader, Hasran Nasrullah, at his office in South Beirut, I was taken to him blindfolded, and the van's driver zigzagged across the city for thirty minutes to confuse me about his location. His bodyguards then spent more than an hour searching me and my equipment. And for years after I first covered a Hezbollah event I would receive a poem on my birthday from their press office.

When I was in Beirut during the spring of 2002, their press attaché called, inviting me to a march that they were organising to protest against "Israeli and Western political oppression." It was to be held at the Fatima Gate, a closed border point between Lebanon and Israel. He assured me that the protest was of extraordinary importance, but when I arrived at the rendezvous, early on a bright, sunny morning, I found the border not only quiet but devoid of people. So I sat in an outdoor café and ordered tea.

It wasn't long before a convoy of buses stopped in front of me and scores of women in black chadors descended onto the tarmac. Two minivans then screeched to a halt, and Hezbollah officials in suits leapt out, opening the doors of the vans to distribute banners and a series of huge canvases among the women. Each painting depicted a member of the pantheon of contemporary Shiite leaders, led by the former spiritual leader of Iran, the Ayatollah Khomeini. The women took the solemn, outsized portraits over to the border fence and waited in a line; they were obviously not discussing the geopolitical situation in the Middle East, however, since all I could hear were giggles and shrieks of laughter.

After ten minutes, one of the Hezbollah officials ran over to the women and ordered them to begin the march. They dutifully picked up the paintings and started to walk along the border fence shouting, "Death to Israel" and "Death to America." Their voices grew louder as they approached the border crossing point, where Israeli troops watched them from a fortified metal tower. At the gate itself, the women bearing portraits turned them towards Israel, as if to threaten an invasion of paintings. The other women came forward and started throwing stones at the tower as the group began to keen. When the missiles hit their target, small pinging noises rang out, adding a percussive tone to the wailing.

Then, as suddenly as it had started, the protest came to an end. The women turned and marched abruptly away, handing the portraits to the men in suits. They climbed into the buses and drove off, leaving me sitting once more, a fresh glass of tea in my hands, listening to that rare commodity in the Middle East—silence.

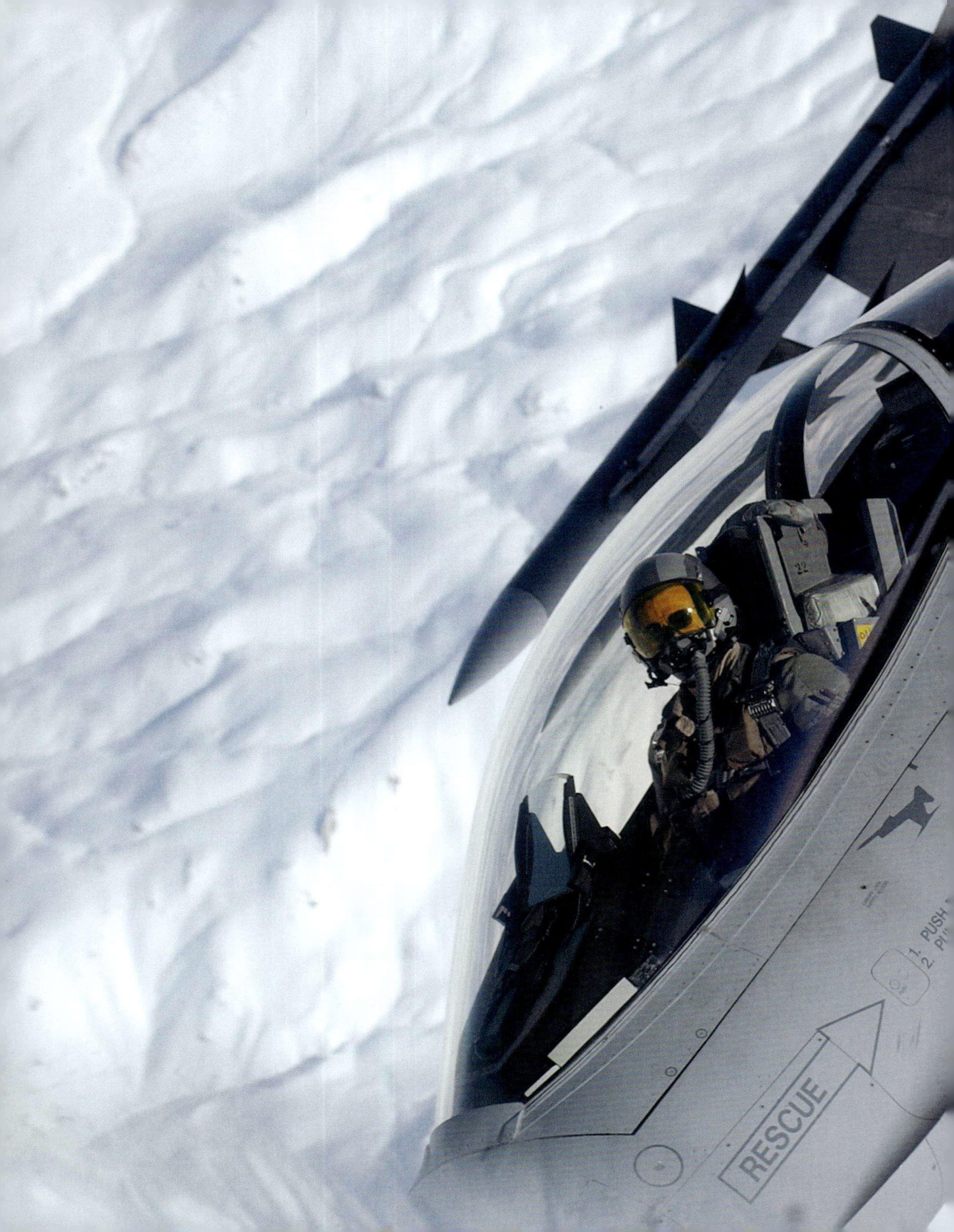
1. PUSH
RESCUE

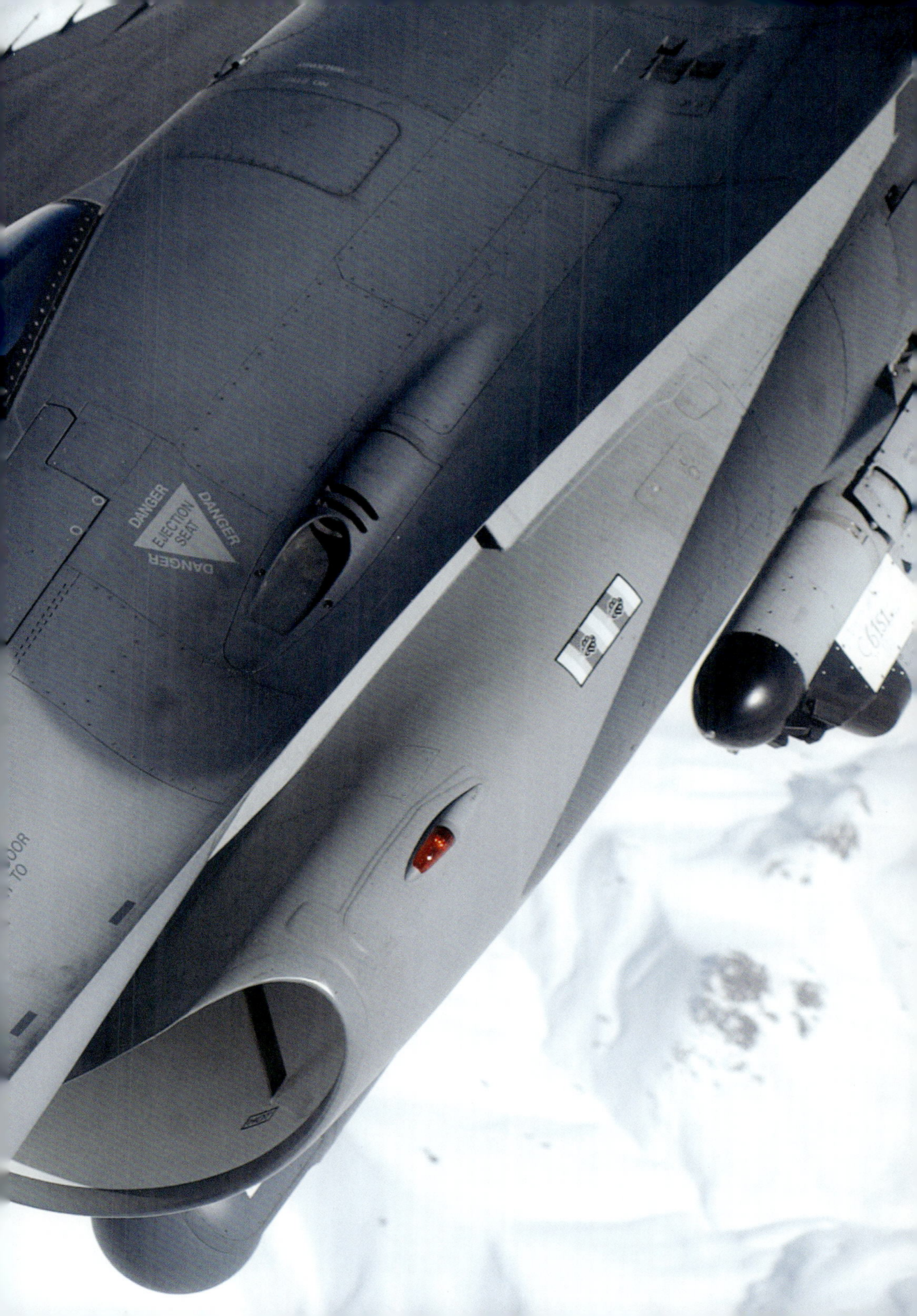
DANGER
EJECTION SEAT
DANGER
DANGER

Operation Northern Watch

Somewhere Over the Turkish-Iraqi Border
22 January 2003

The airman who was lying next to me on a pane of glass above the snowy Quandil Mountains of the Turkish-Iraqi border was bored with filling fighter planes with kerosene at thirty thousand feet. His job was, admittedly, simple: to extend the aerial-refuelling craft's boom to the fighter planes stacked in the sky around us and then press a button to release fuel down a hose. The pilots, who flew extraordinarily close for refuelling, would normally enliven his shift by flashing him centrefolds from *Playboy*. On this particular day, however, they had refrained, perhaps because of my presence, and that did not improve his mood.

In 2003, as thousands of troops massed in the Arabian Gulf, Operation Northern Watch—the mission imposing a no-fly zone, above the 36th parallel, on Saddam Hussein after the first Gulf War—was coming to an end. The aerial patrols' central purpose had been to stop Saddam from attacking the Kurds, and from this perspective they had been a success. Militarily, however, the exchanges were less like war than like a potentially lethal game of cat-and-mouse: the Iraqis would fire on the Allied aircraft but always miss; the pilots would then retaliate, but the U.S. became so worried about civilian casualties that its planes began dropping bombs made of concrete instead of explosives.

From our glass platform at the rear of the KC-135 Stratotanker, the snow-white peaks of Kurdistan passed like a postcard below and the fighter planes, framed against the mountains, seemed more like toys than like machines of destruction.

A dozen F-15s and F-16s came in to refuel before their descent into Iraq. They hovered so tightly off the tail of the tanker that I was afraid they would crash into us during one of the interminable pockets of turbulence that complicated their approach, but every manoeuvre passed off without a hitch. After several hours, I, too, had grown weary of watching these jets engaged in such a remarkable yet mundane operation when one pilot pulled back and dived past us at full throttle.

I swivelled on the glass to catch him before he vanished, unsure whether to be angry or amused when I found him staring back at me, posing for a second before he resumed his routine.

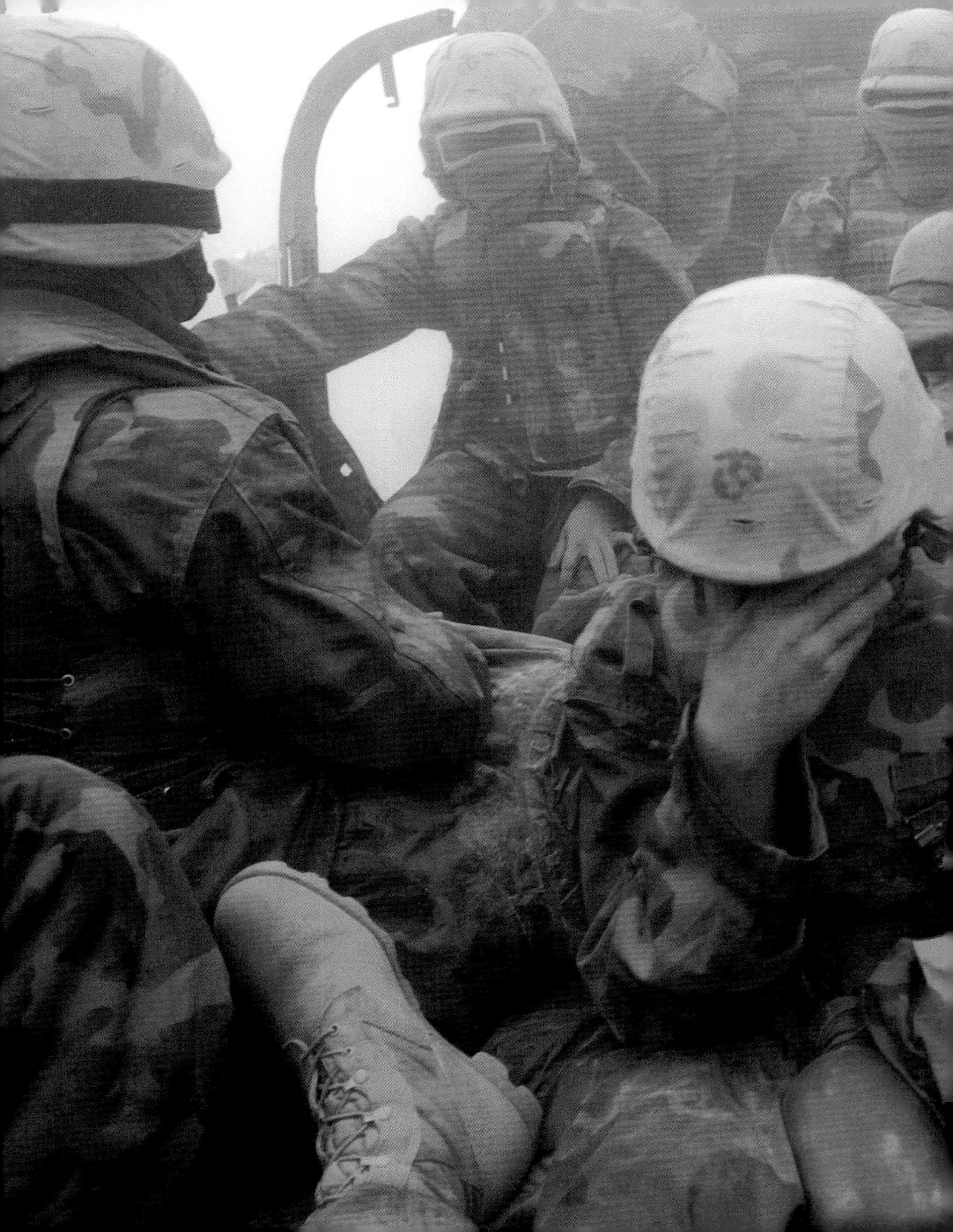

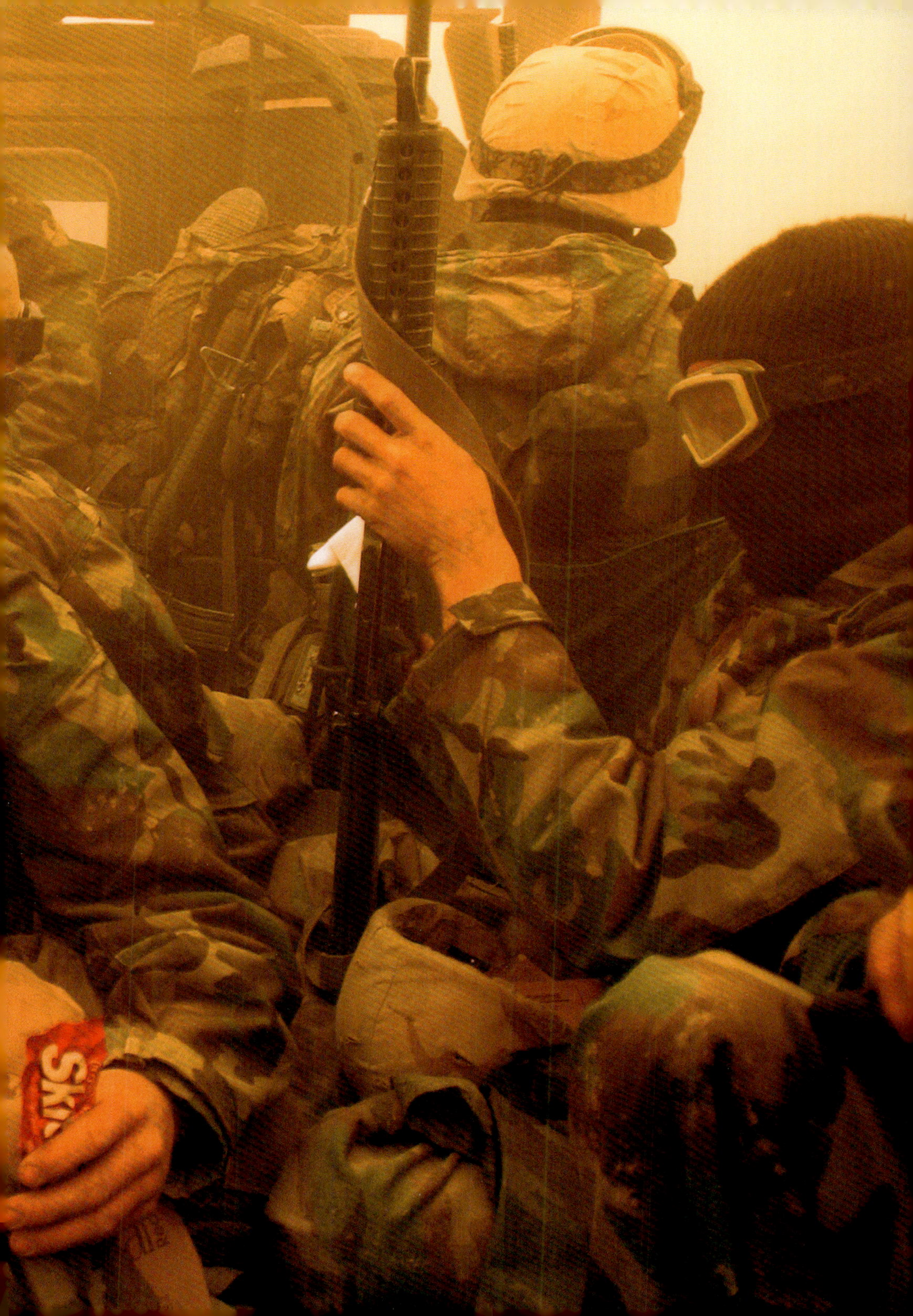

Skittles

Al Zubair Desert, Iraq
25 March 2003

The desert in southern Iraq is a bleak landscape with few dunes and only the occasional ball of tumbleweed to enliven its interminable flatness. When, a week into the invasion of Iraq, a storm engulfed the Marine convoy with which I was travelling, I felt as if I were drowning in a red mist of blandness.

Until the storm, the Allied advance had met with little resistance. American forces had breezed through Safwan, a town on the Kuwaiti-Iraqi border, and then headed north through Nasiriyah, crossing the Euphrates into the desert. If first the troops had battled an invisible army, now only the weather seemed ready to oppose them.

Equipped for the beach rather than for the desert, the Marine Expeditionary Force added to the fantastical air of the campaign. Their vehicles, intended for amphibious landings, resembled a long line of stranded whales that had taken a wrong turn. Legend proclaimed that we were close to the Garden of Eden, but there was nothing but a barren horizon to greet us.

The night before the storm, I had spoken to a sergeant from White Sulphur Springs, West Virginia, who bemoaned the lack of fast-food outlets on the highway through the desert. The Marines and I were surviving on one pack of MREs (Meals Ready to Eat) per day, instead of the regulation two.

An MRE pack consisted of a main course chosen from one of twenty-four recipes, many of which, such at Chicken Tetrazzini, were largely unknown to the wider culinary world. In addition, there were crackers, cookies, jam, peanut butter, cheese spread, candies, and—mercifully—hot-pepper sauce to disguise the taste of all of the above.

The ferocity of the storm did not improve the Marines' lot. Most of the troops were sheltered inside their amphibious vehicles, but some units were travelling in open trucks and had nowhere to hide. Hour after hour, as the wind howled and the sand cut their faces, the Marines merely sat there, bundled up like mummies, lost in their thoughts. Even my camera became disoriented, tingeing photographs with a Hadean shade of red as the white balance went haywire trying to make sense of the colours of the whirling sandstorm.

At one point, I found a Marine sitting in front of me eating his Skittles, holding the pack as if he were clinging to the last vestige of civilisation before being swallowed by the storm. For some, the picture became emblematic of the dislocation of the war, and it was used for one of the covers of Thomas E. Ricks' book "Fiasco," an examination of the U.S. military adventure in Iraq. The packet of Skittles had to be darkened, though, in order to avoid unauthorised use of the Skittles brand.

By dawn, the wind had eased and we had edged a few precious miles closer to Baghdad when a small group of Iraqi soldiers ambushed us. The Marines, after being hemmed in for a whole day, sprang into action, dispatching most of the enemy within a minute. The men who survived and surrendered turned out to be middle-aged and poorly armed; many of them claimed to have been press-ganged into fighting. They hadn't stood a chance, and were simply glad to be alive.

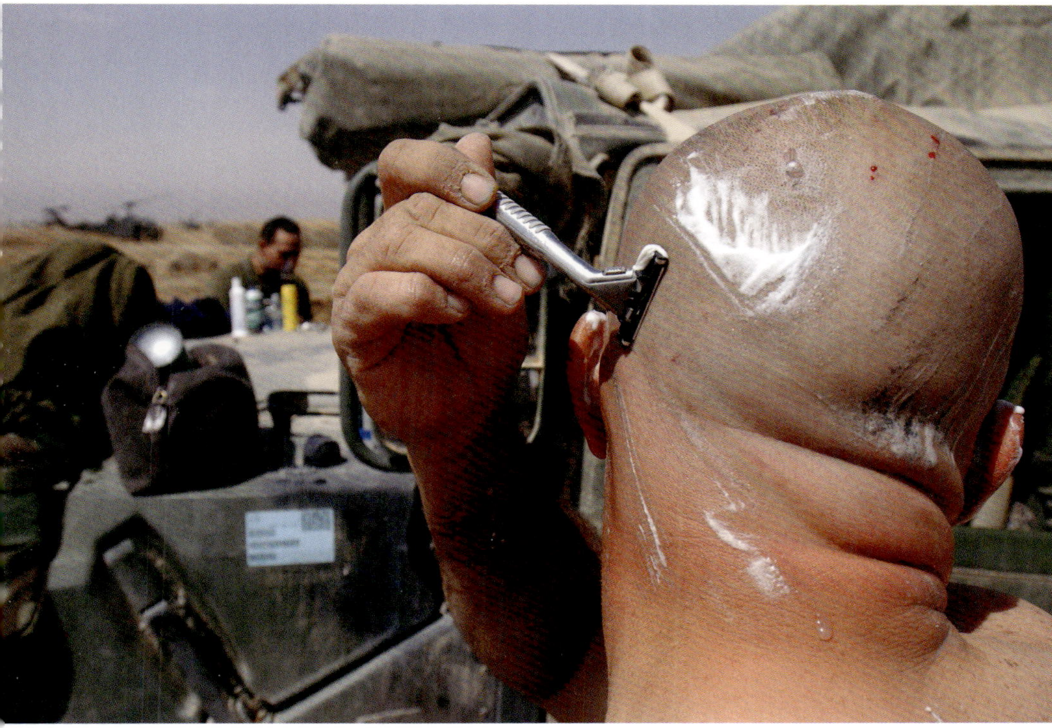

The Operational Pause

Southern Iraq
29 March 2003

A week into the invasion of Iraq, the armoured, amphibious columns of Marines came to a halt. Colonel John Pomfret, the commander of the unit with which I had just unofficially been embedded, described it as an "operational pause." As far as I could make out, we had simply stopped in the middle of the desert.

It was by chance that I was travelling with the U.S. Marines at all. The first day of the war, Dexter Filkins and I had managed to cross the border into Iraq in a rented jeep by flashing a military pass that I had picked up from a Kuwaiti Army colonel in a hotel lobby in Kuwait City. But after three days in the desert, we had run out of food and water as well as people to photograph. Then we found the Marines, who kindly let us tag along.

Of all the military forces I have known, rarely have I encountered such a strange mix of civility and ferocity as I found amongst the Marines. They were unfailingly polite and, despite my being a journalist, always addressed me as "Sir." Friendly relations were also helped by the fact that I could barter calls to the U.S. on my satellite phone for all kinds of government property.

One incident during the journey to Baghdad remains especially vivid. As we were drawing closer to the Iraqi capital, we came upon two farmers in a pickup truck who had strayed too close to the Marine lines. They were ordered to stop, and obeyed instantly; even if they had no knowledge of English, the twenty M16 rifles pointing at them made the command unmistakable. But the driver, whether out of fear or by accident, had left the truck in gear. After a tense pause, it lurched forwards, and the Marines, already on edge, unleashed a deafening barrage of gunfire into the engine. The farmers, unhurt, stumbled out of the cabin, looking with bewilderment first at their truck and then at their assailants. As the engine burst into flames, one of them started to weep, unable to comprehend how his world had been so suddenly upended.

Against my expectations, I grew fond of our travelling companions. Yet it astonished me that even the mundane task of shaving could carry such undertones of violence. Surely this Marine could feel these cuts as he made them, but he never flinched. The beads of blood stood proudly on the top of his head like a badge of honour until he eventually took a towel and wiped them off.

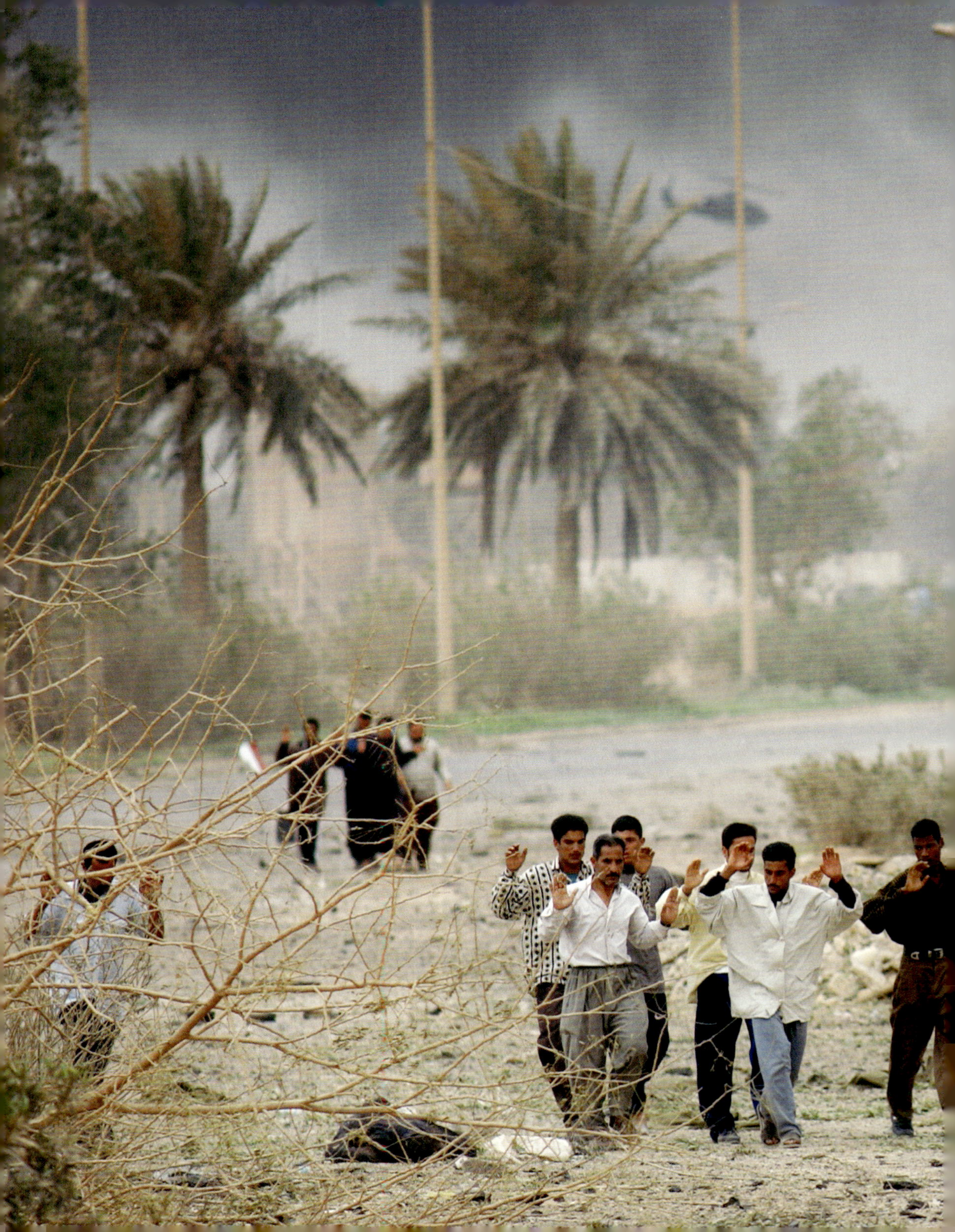

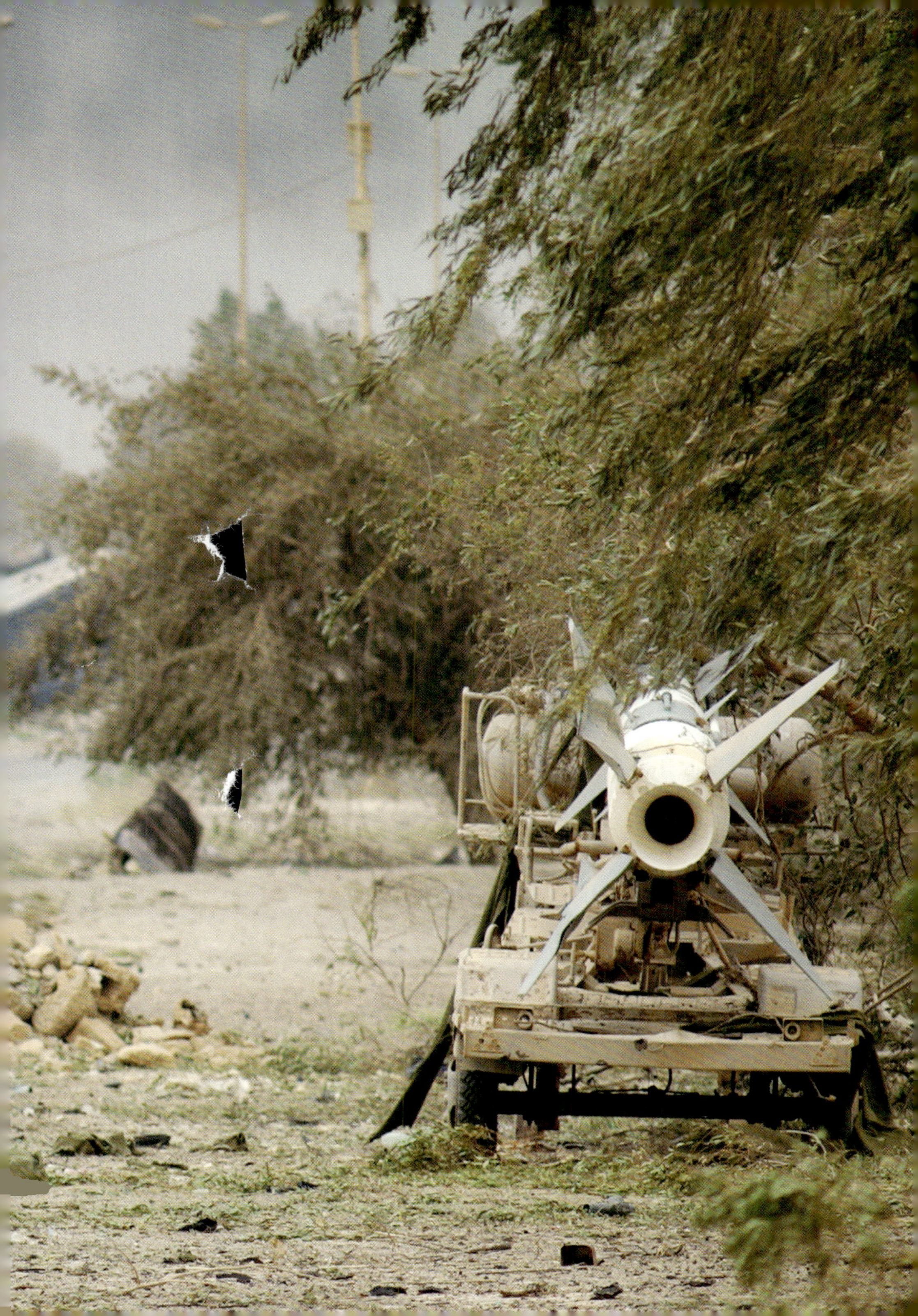

The Unintentional Avant-Garde

Diyala Bridge, Baghdad
8 April 2003

I woke up to the smell of rotting meat. When I opened the tent, I found a flattened dog barely two metres away. I couldn't understand how I had failed to see it the night before, but the corpse was a reminder of the chaotic experience of entering Baghdad with the Marines the previous day.

On 7 April, after two weeks in the desert embedded with various Marine units, my colleague Dexter Filkins and I had reached the bridge over the Diyala River, the city's last natural defence, and persuaded a Marine colonel to let us cross it with his lead units. We quickly found ourselves and our yellow Hertz rental jeep at the forefront of the Marines' attack on the Iraqi capital.

If this was a journalistic coup it was also, quite clearly, a very bad idea. And yet the wisdom of retreating eluded us. Although the streets were deserted, the presence of an enemy was tangible, and occasional bursts of fire would pepper the lead vehicles. At one point, we encountered a burning Iraqi ammunition truck spitting bullets, but we managed to shield ourselves behind an armoured amphibious vehicle and passed it unscathed.

As darkness fell, the column pushed deeper into the city and we became increasingly vulnerable: unlike the Marines, we had no night-vision goggles. Dexter hunched over the wheel like a little old lady, peering at the blackened horizon illuminated only by the occasional burst of tank or machine-gun fire. After an hour, the convoy halted in no-man's-land and our predicament was ended by the reappearance of the colonel, who informed us, in brusque military terms, that our presence was no longer desired and that we were to return immediately to Diyala Bridge. We haltingly retraced our steps, pitched our tent in utter darkness—it was forbidden by the Marines to use any white light—and crawled inside to file our story and our pictures.

The next morning, I awoke before Dexter and found the dog.

Looking beyond its corpse, I saw that the situation around us had changed dramatically since we crossed the bridge the day before. A Marine command post had sprung up next to us, overlooking a battle that was now unfolding on the near horizon. Beyond an abandoned missile—possibly one of those which we had feared would launch a chemical bombardment—a Cobra helicopter went into the attack. Sporadic gunfire punctured the early-morning calm, and vast plumes of smoke billowed from burning oil depots, thickening the air so heavily that each breath tasted of tar.

Slowly, cautiously, a group of Iraqi men walked towards the Marine position, their hands in the air. It was unclear whether they were civilians or soldiers who had abandoned their uniforms to blend in with the crowd. At one point, one of them paused to regard a corpse as if recognizing someone he knew, before deciding that it was not worth a closer inspection and resuming his passage.

I felt that I had stumbled onto a movie set: the scene and its props seemed too precisely placed, and I doubted their veracity. Only when a Marine standing next to me barked out commands to the Iraqis trudging towards us did I come to my senses and realize that the fall of Baghdad might be imminent. I poked my head into the tent and begged Dexter to get up.

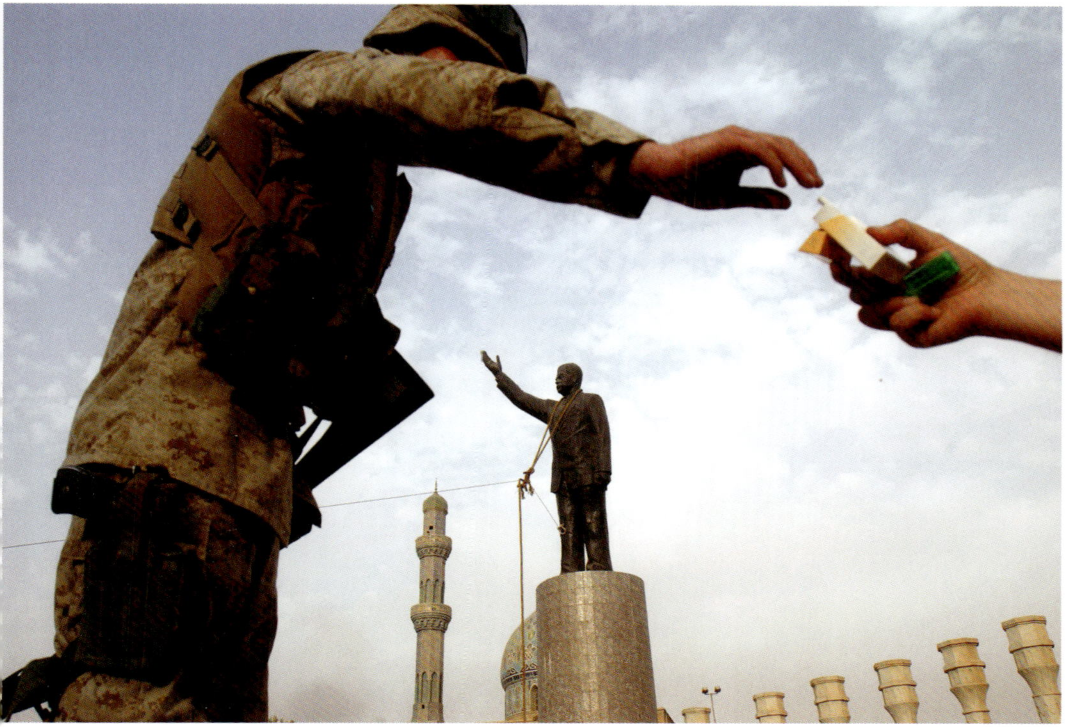

A False Freedom

Firdooz Square, Baghdad
9 April 2003

There were probably hundreds of statues of Saddam Hussein in Baghdad in April 2003, but there was only one in front of CNN's live position. And so it was in Firdooz Square that the fall of Saddam Hussein's regime symbolically took place.

I had arrived in the square early in the afternoon, after driving through a city that was plunged into chaos. Government buildings were burning everywhere and looters flocked to the streets, rifling through any office or shop, filling their arms so high that they were unable to see in front of them.

The war, such as it was, seemed over. Although there had never really been any doubt that Saddam would be toppled and pushed from Baghdad, the question had remained whether or not he would use the chemical weapons that were the rationale for the invasion.

During the march to Baghdad, the existence of these weapons had seemed very real. When, several days into the invasion, the alarm sounded for an incoming gas attack, I was deeply afraid. I had a gas mask and an antidote-filled syringe, but that morning I had forgotten to shave, and for the mask to perfectly seal my face I needed to be clean-shaven. So I sat there in a tent with a group of Marines, trying to breathe calmly though my respirator and fingering the syringe in my pocket as sweat dripped down the inside of my mask. I thought of my ten-month-old son and my pregnant wife. No one said a word as we waited, listening; the noise of our respirators made us sound like a Darth Vader convention that had taken a wrong turn into the desert. Each of the three alarms that night turned out to be false, but the threat of chemical weapons stayed with us; even if I had doubted the legal or political justification of the invasion, it was with considerable relief that I reached the centre of the Iraqi capital that afternoon.

When I first approached Firdooz Square, a group of Iraqi men who had climbed onto the statue were beating it with their shoes, the most degrading of Arab insults. Still, it was a small crowd, and when an American tank-rescue truck arrived a few hours later and put a rope around Saddam's neck, there were as many journalists as soldiers or Iraqis standing around the monument. Although I sensed that this was a moment of history, my instinct also told me to retreat, which is when I took this photograph of an Iraqi offering a Marine a cigarette—in precisely what spirit, it was hard to say.

Moments afterwards, the truck reversed, but the rope snapped under the strain. So the crew replaced it with a thick metal chain, and ripped Saddam Hussein right off his pedestal. A few months later, the real war in Iraq began.

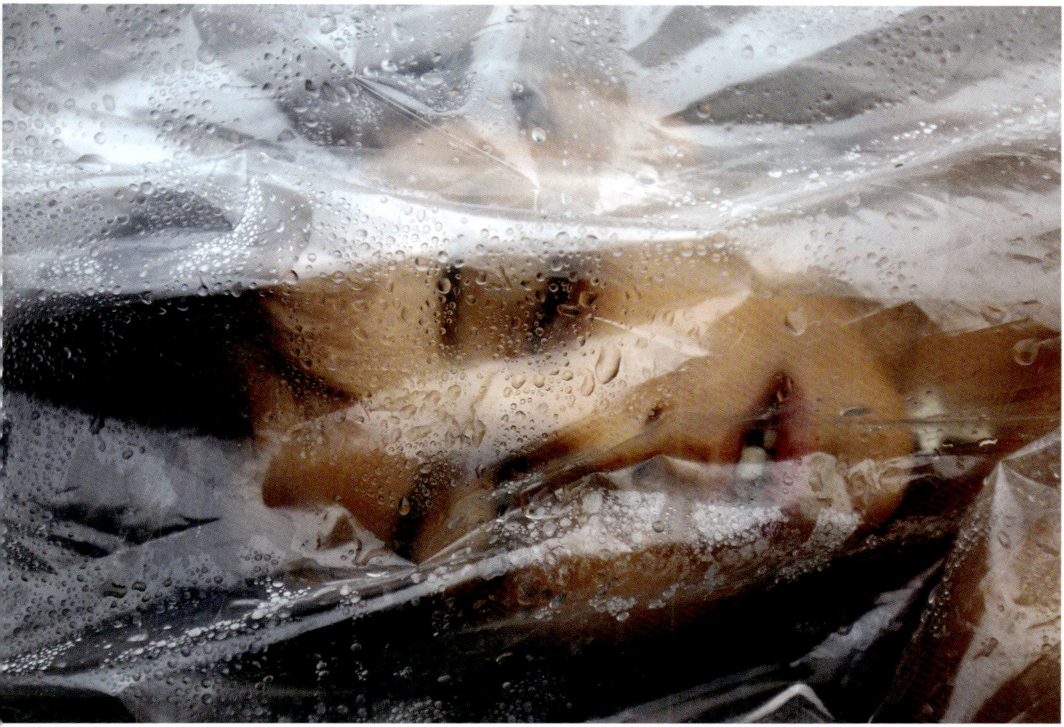

Every time I look at the boy, I tell myself that he is sleeping. But this illusion can hold for only so long.

When Chechen terrorists captured School No. 1 in the town of Beslan, in the North Caucasus, on the first day of term, 1 September 2004, I was in France. The next day, I flew to Moscow, and the day after that to Ossetia. But as the flight was about land in Beslan the plane suddenly regained height and a stewardess announced that we were being diverted to Mineralnye Vody, two hundred kilometres to the west. A hush fell over the plane. Everyone on board, many of them relatives of the hostages, knew that something terrible had happened. As we were to find out later, Russian Special Forces had just stormed the school.

I took a taxi in Mineralnye Vody and began the long drive to Beslan. The news on the radio was so incoherent that it was completely unclear what had happened. There were checkpoints everywhere, and as we came closer to Beslan the police were increasingly nervous. A torrential downpour occurred as I arrived in the city, leaving the streets almost deserted. Only when I reached my colleague's apartment and saw the shock on the faces of the people with whom I was staying did I begin to understand the scale of the tragedy. More than three hundred people had died in the battle between the terrorists and the Special Forces, and more than half of the casualties were children.

The Innocents

Vladikavkaz, North Ossetia
5 September 2004

The following morning brought the hideous aftermath. The school was closed off for investigation. The first funerals were held. Many of those who were known to have been inside the school were still missing, and relatives began a frantic search for them. First they went to the hospitals; if that proved fruitless, then they went, in resignation, to the morgues.

When I drove to the nearby city of Vladikavkaz, a day later, I found more than a hundred victims lying, unclaimed, in the courtyard of its morgue; the main building was too small to accommodate the surfeit of corpses.

The dead were divided into two sections. On the side of the yard closest to the building lay the victims who were visibly maimed or burnt. When the storming of the school began, the ceiling of the gym where the students and the parents were being held caught fire. The burning beams had fallen onto the hostages and many of them had been horribly disfigured during the panic that ensued. Those bodies, bloated and oozing, lay inside foil and thick black plastic. As relatives peeled back the plastic, looking for their missing family members, they recoiled from the sight of the misshapen torsos and from the overpowering stench.

On the other side of the yard lay the victims whose bodies were relatively unharmed—some didn't seem damaged at all—wrapped in transparent sheeting. The plastic was speckled with drops of rain from the previous night.

Watching the relatives warily circle the courtyard, I could sense their apprehension and uncertainty; they dreaded finding their loved ones, but also dreaded failing to do so. Every few minutes a terrible shriek of grief would rend the silence, shredding everyone's nerves still further. I wandered in a daze, struggling, vainly, to absorb the scale of distress. I found it impossible not to stare at the children, searching their faces as if I were watching my own children asleep. I stepped lightly between their delicate frames, afraid to disturb them in any way, although I knew it would make no difference. Then I found the boy. Even among so many angelic faces, there was a magnetic quality about him. I took a few pictures of him and then paused, puzzled by the missing tooth visible in his open mouth. I wondered, like a curious father, if it was a baby tooth that had fallen out before the tragedy, or if it had been knocked out in some other way.

And then, unable to look any longer, I turned and walked out the gate.

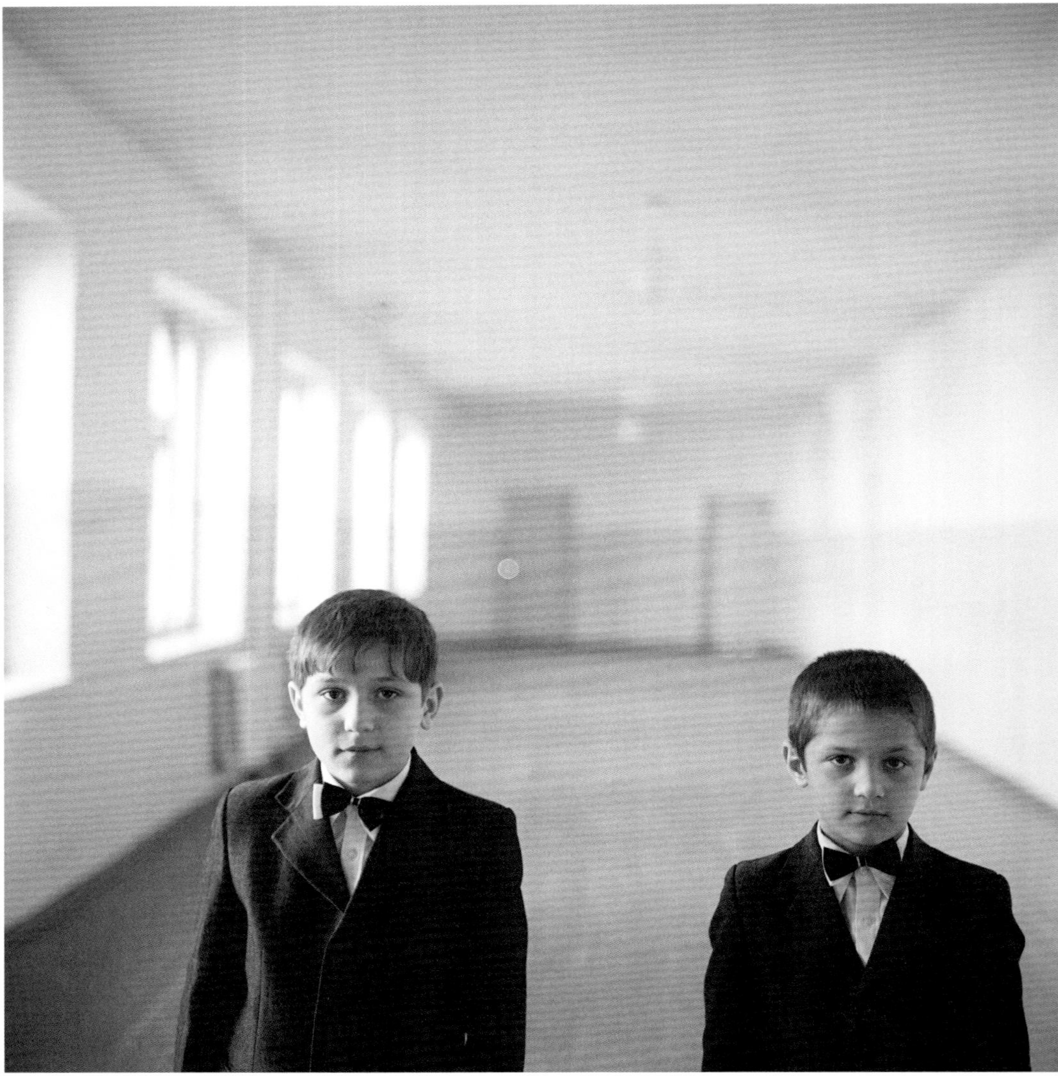

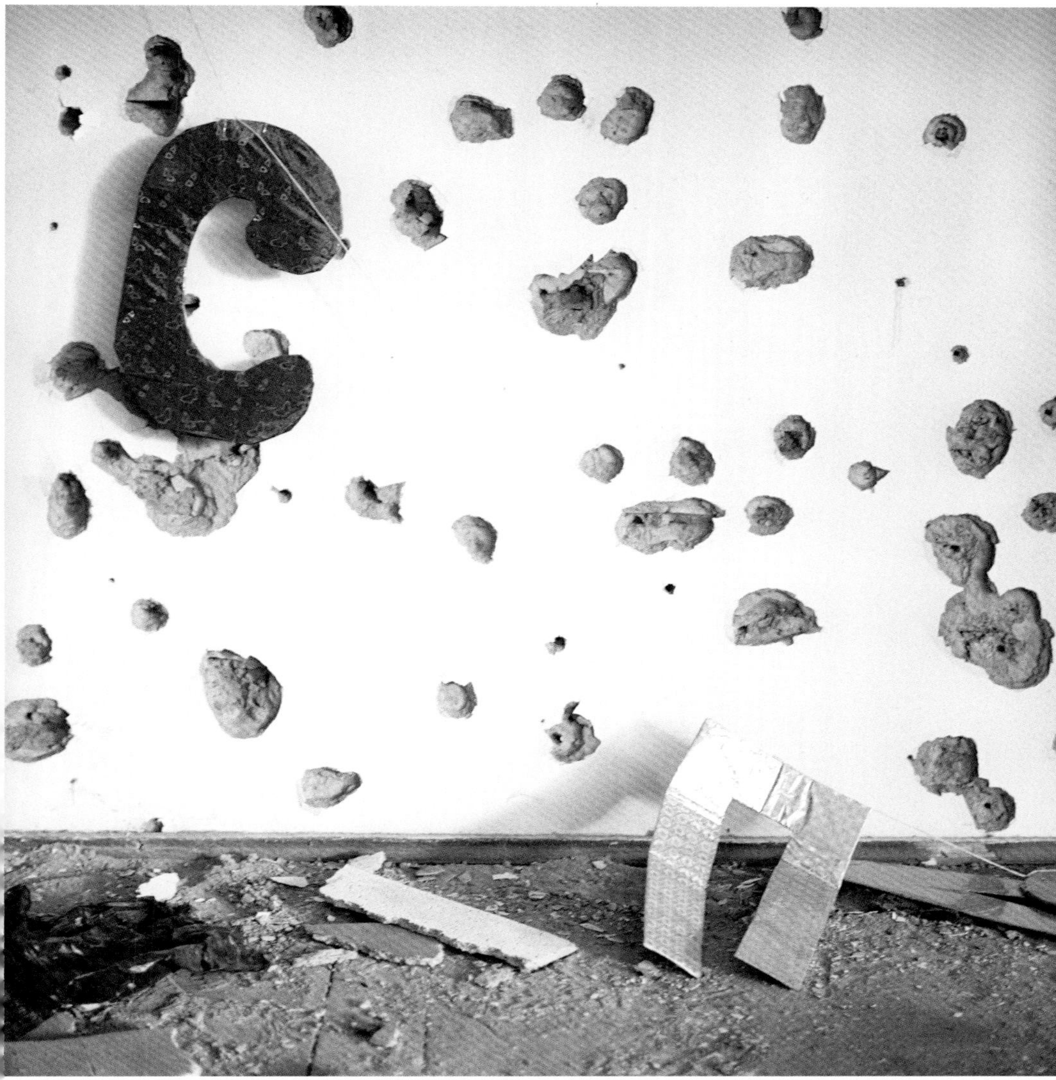

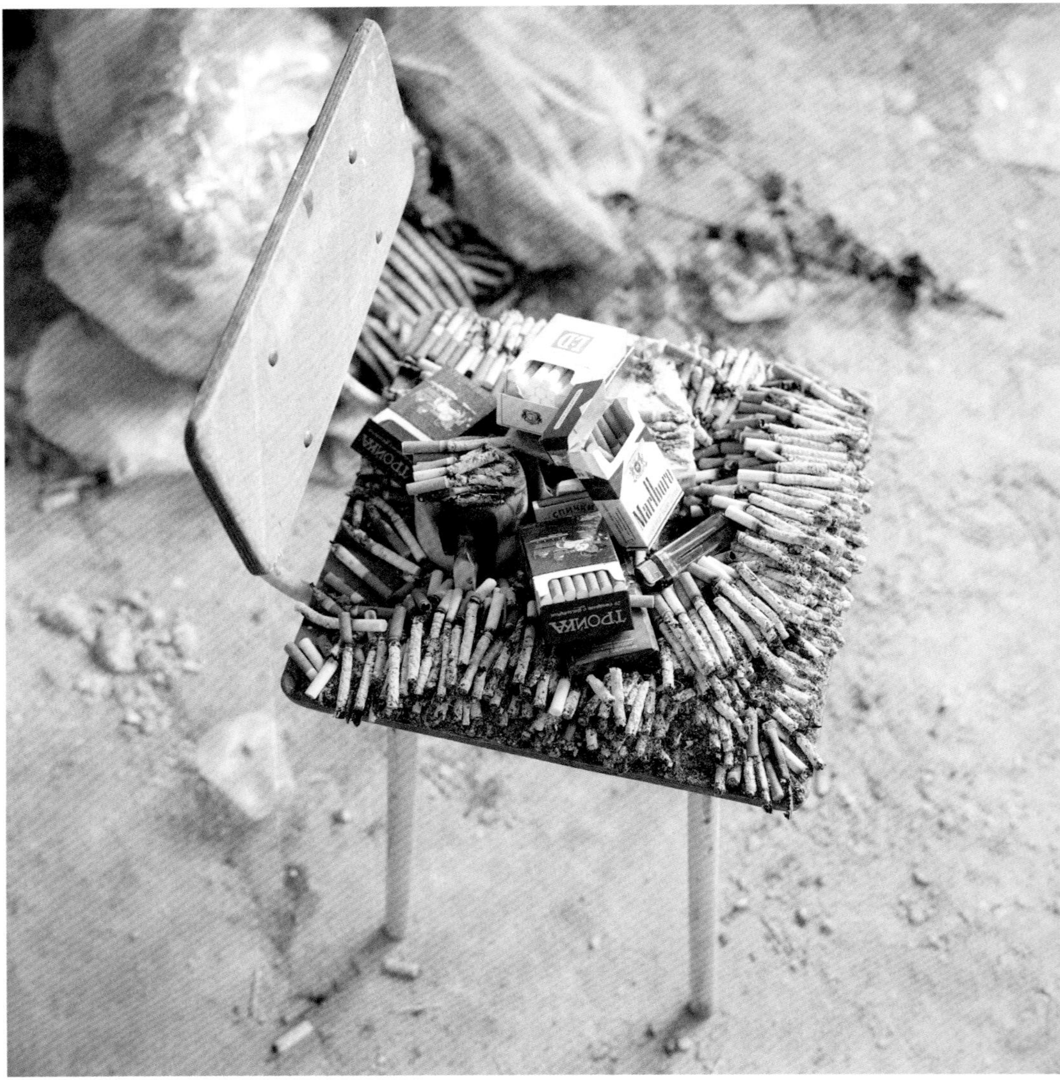
ТРОЙКА
Marlboro
СПИЧКИ
ТРОЙКА

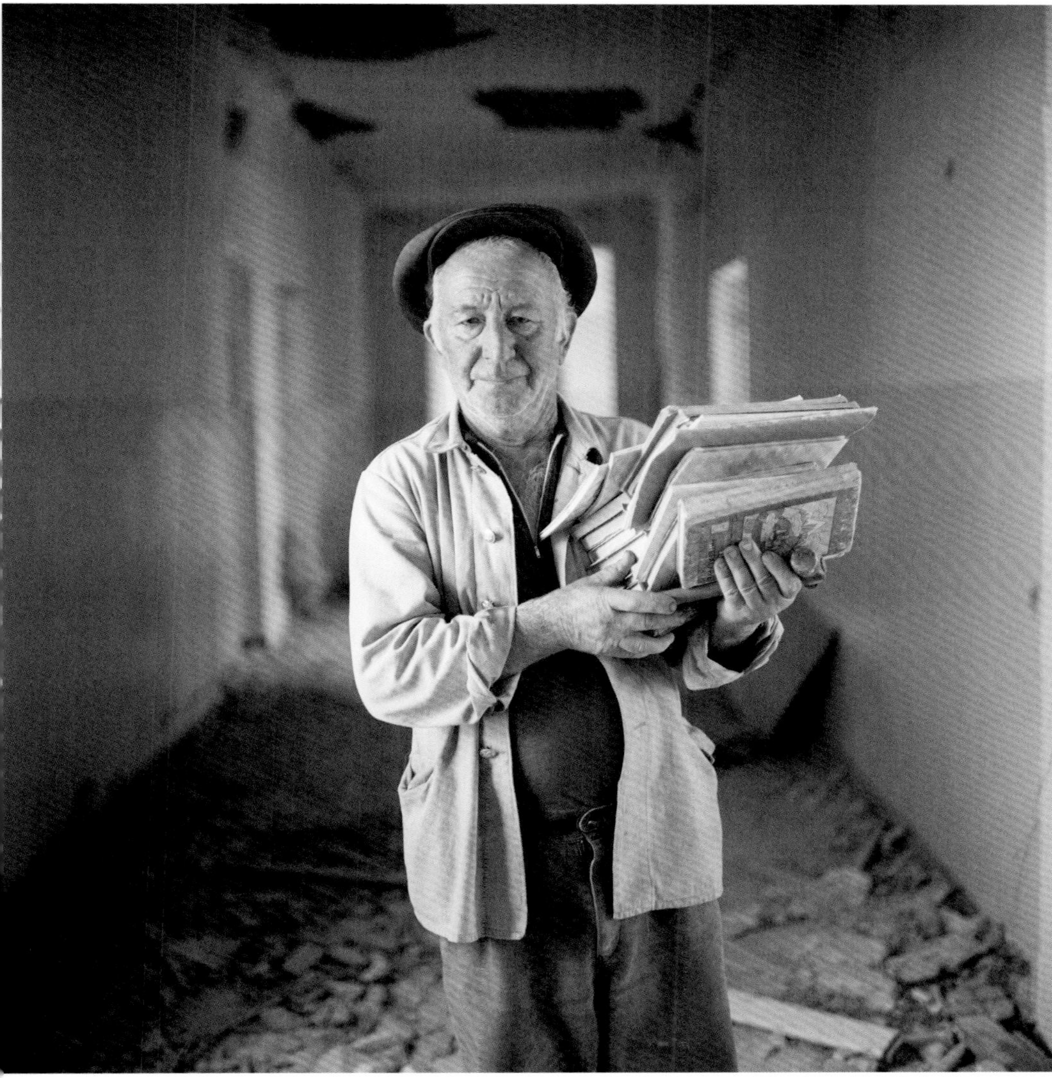

After

Beslan, North Ossetia
September 2004

I went back to Beslan two weeks after the tragedy, when the local authorities decided to reopen the schools, in a futile effort to return to normalcy.

If one of the unwritten laws of conduct in war is that women and children should not be targeted, then everyone in Beslan knew that a line had been crossed and a moral compass shattered. The people of the town were bereaved not only of their children but also of their belief in humanity's inherent goodness.

People did not know how to express their grief with words, so they tried, instead, with actions. They turned School No. 1, the site of the tragedy, into a shrine. Rather than shying away, relatives and visitors flocked to its battle-scarred corridors, as if it were imperative to face their horror.

People brought bottles of water—the hostages had been deprived of water while they were held in the school gym—and biscuits and sweets: they had been refused food as well. There were also mountains of flowers, cuddly toys, and religious icons, as if a sea of compassion could somehow obliterate what had taken place there. One man salvaged books, as if knowledge itself could be rescued. In a classroom on the first floor, the terrorists had systematically shot and then thrown out of the window all the children's male relatives, to remove any physical threat from inside the building. Here local Ossetian men lit dozens of cigarettes and left them to burn on a chair as a mark of respect for these victims' sacrifice.

Several hundred metres from School No. 1, at School No. 6, where the surviving pupils had been reassigned, the corridors echoed with the steps of those children who had been brave enough to attend. Parents kept guard on the porch, armed with shotguns and rifles. When classes started, the teachers had no idea where to begin, so they asked the students to draw. The children put pen to paper and sketched semi-naked pupils, their hands held behind the backs of their heads, being watched over by masked men with rifles.

As I walked down the silent streets of Beslan on that sunny morning, I heard screams, although there were none, and at several points I began to cry uncontrollably.

One man I visited had lost his wife and their only child, a ten-year-old girl. Still, every morning he set the breakfast table for three. Then he cleared everything away again. All that remained were his memories and an album filled with faded photographs.

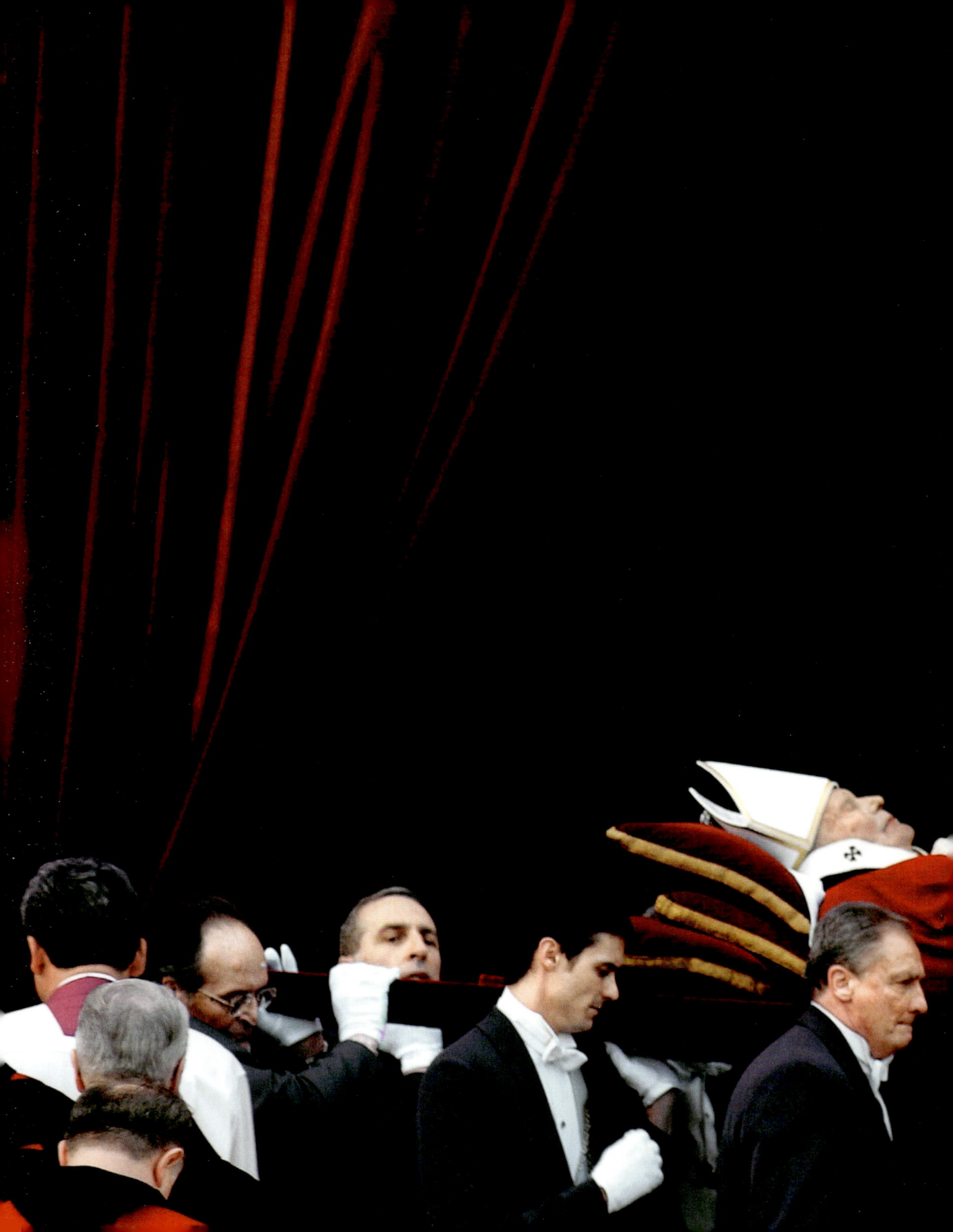

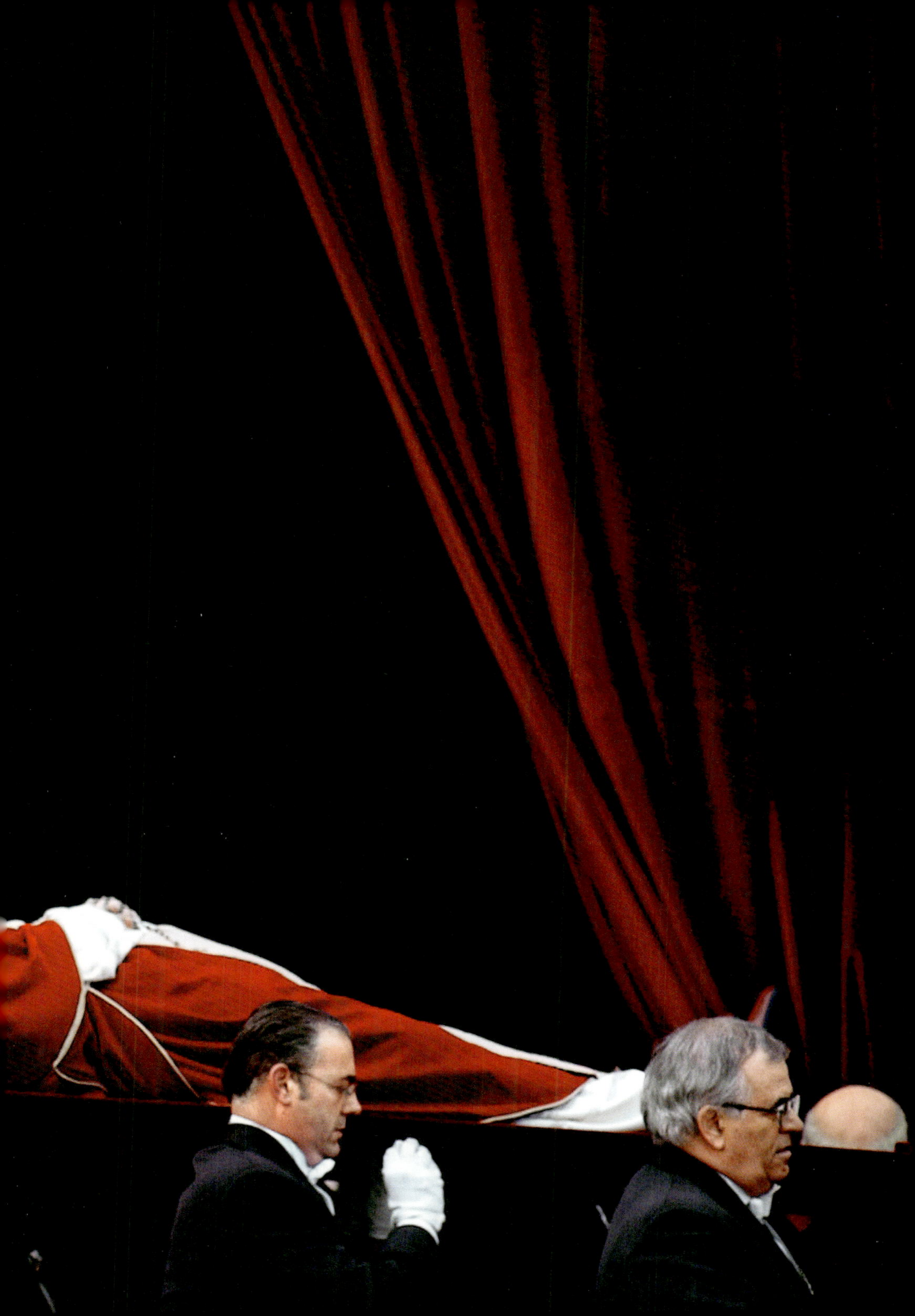

Death of the Pope

Rome

4 April 2005

We had been standing there for hours; still, it felt indecent to be waiting so impatiently for a corpse. When the gentlemen of the Vatican finally appeared in their long morning coats, carrying Pope John Paul II on their shoulders, the crowd was unsure how to react. Some people remained silent, as if in awe; others cried out the Holy Father's name, as if he were still alive. Most simply busied themselves taking photographs on their mobile phones as the Pope bobbed in and out view, his bright-crimson shoes cutting a vivid passage through the crowd.

I was directly in front of the entrance of St. Peter's, watching the cortège's unhurried approach. Tracking the patricians through a long lens, I could see beads of sweat appear on their foreheads as the weight of the body and the bier began to tire their arms. While I waited, I mentally rehearsed the moment when they would cross in front of me, envisioning the photograph I would take. But when they finally marched past, so close that I could almost reach out and touch the Pope, the scene suddenly became uninteresting—as if proximity had stolen the body's dignity. The procession moved away, mounting the steep incline in front of the basilica and carrying my confusion with it.

In despair, I watched the cortège arrive at the curtained entrance of St. Peter's. Here, without warning, the gentlemen-in-waiting paused and turned sideways. As they manoeuvred to show John Paul II's body to the crowd one last time, the face, the mitre, and the enrobed body of the Pope were fleetingly silhouetted against the darkened interior.

The cortège disappeared into the basilica a moment later and I smiled. Even in death, John Paul II—who had astonished papal crowds on so many occasions—had the kindness to spring one last surprise, and I thanked him for his gift.

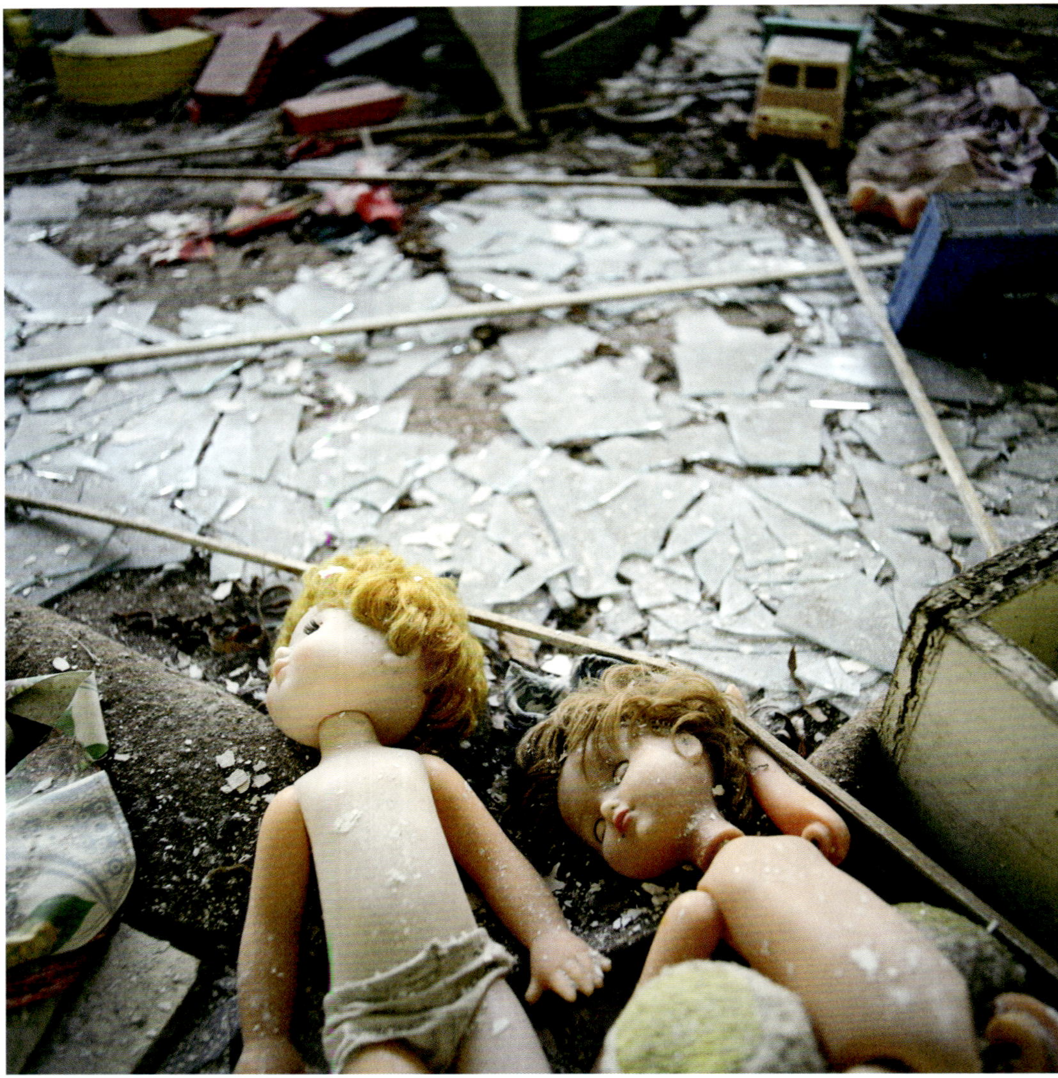

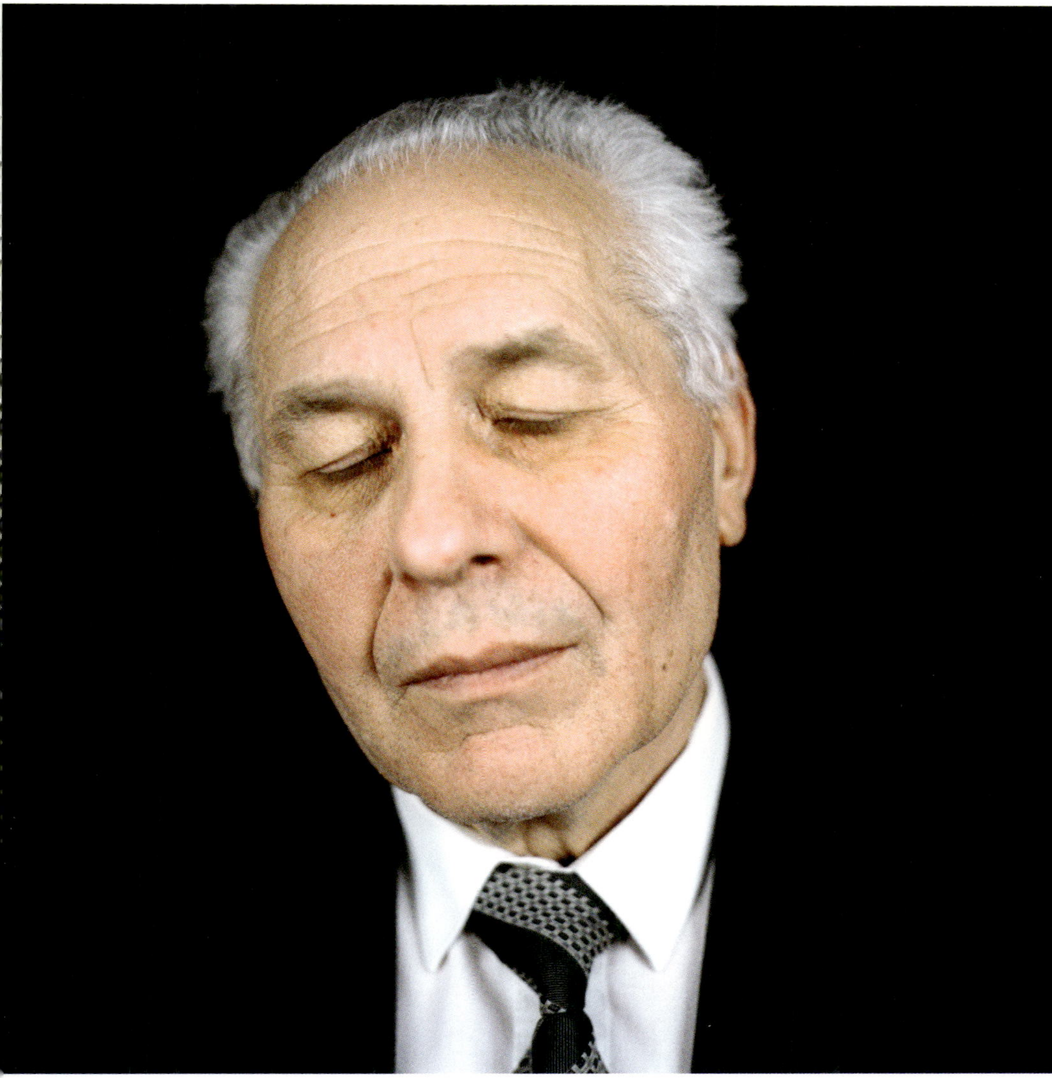

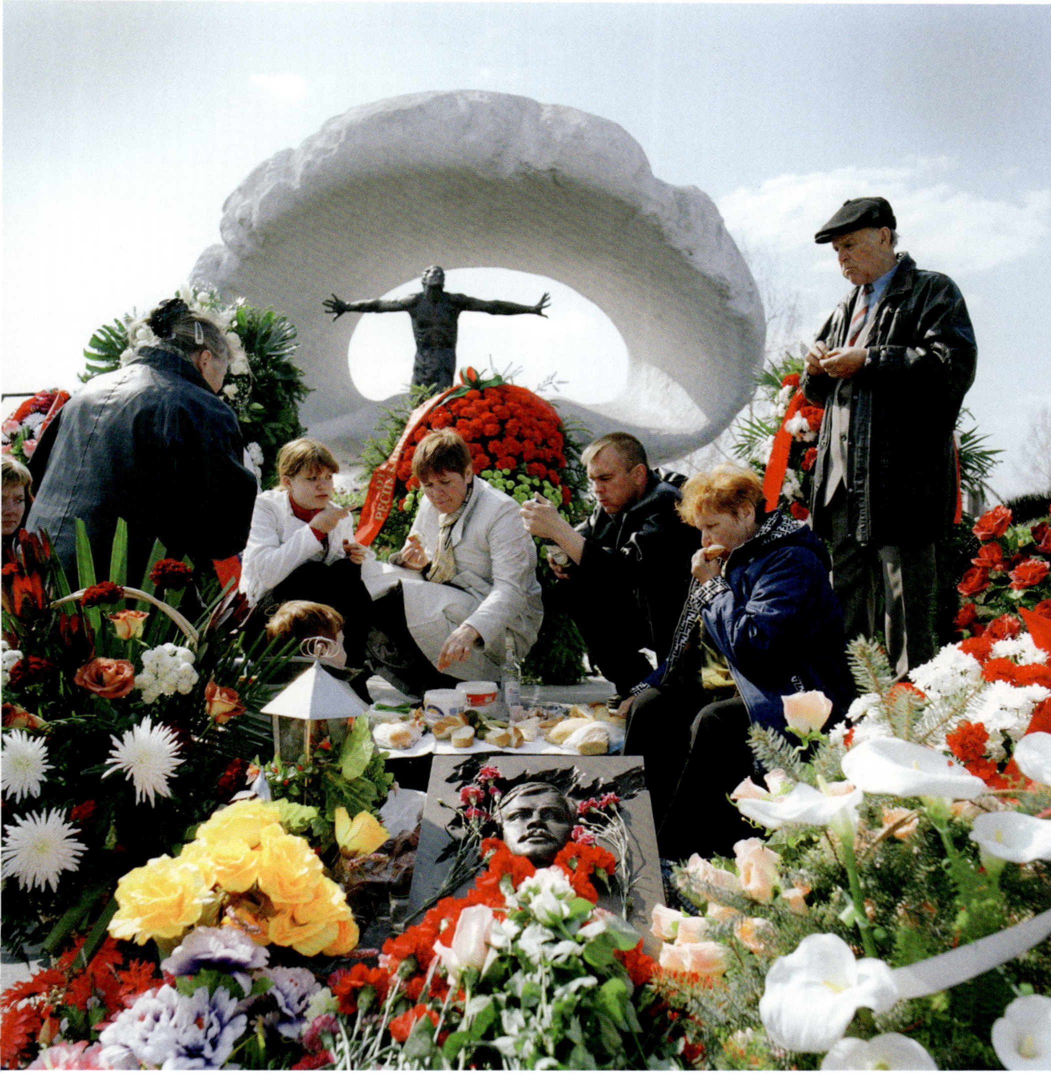

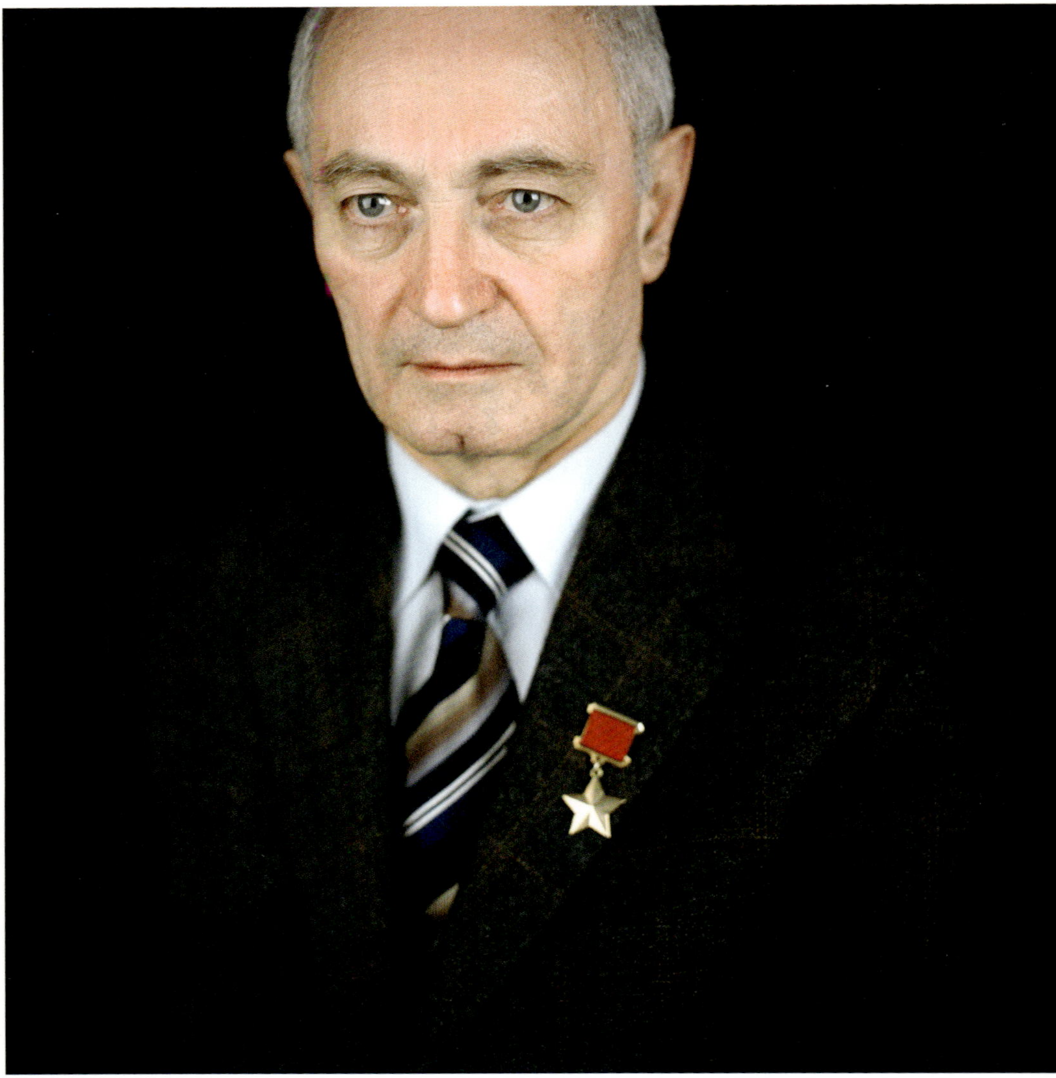

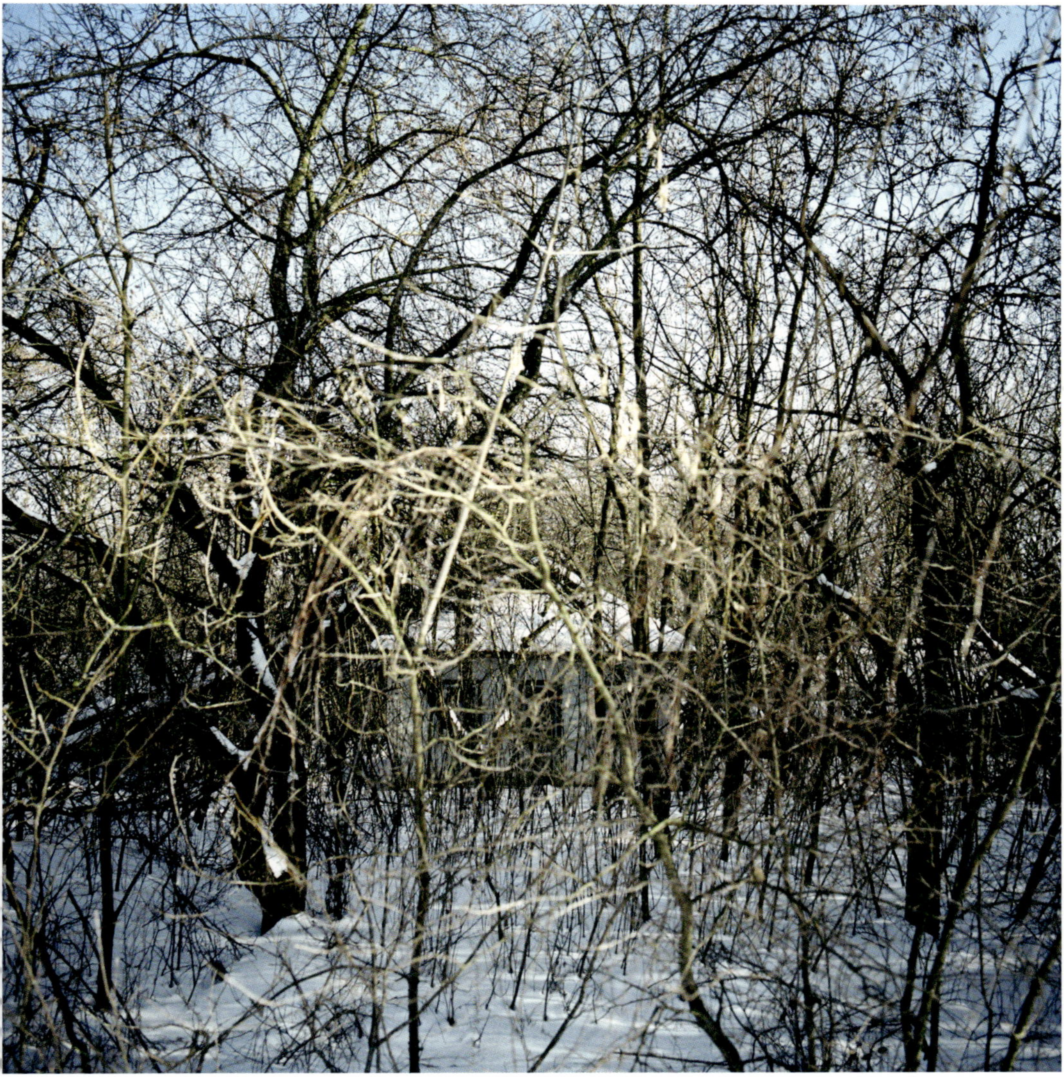

The Invisible War

The Chernobyl Zone and the Liquidators

April 2006

Chernobyl became part of my life in 1991, when I arrived to live in Kiev, the Ukrainian capital, where it was impossible not to feel the rawness of the city's wounds. Almost every ache and ailment was blamed upon the nuclear accident, which had occurred only eighty kilometres away, and its shadow seeped into me invisibly and irresistibly, just as the plant's radiation had penetrated the bones of its workers.

The population's continued fear and anger were understandable. In the days after the fire broke out at the fourth reactor at Chernobyl, on 26 April 1986, the Communist Party leaders behaved like cowards and liars. Plant workers and their families watched radioactive particles spew out of the reactor like fireworks for twenty-four hours before they were finally evacuated. And, in Kiev itself, the traditional celebration of the workers' holiday of 1 May went forward as planned; people thronged the streets even as a radioactive cloud blanketed the city.

Each journey to Chernobyl and the thirty-kilometre exclusion zone that surrounded it required official permission. When I planned my first visit there, a month after my arrival, I asked my translator, Sasha, to accompany me. Out of loyalty, he agreed, and, to combat the anticipated radiation, he started a course of potions based on local wives' tales. The morning of our departure, however, he failed to show up, and, while I understood almost none of the official explanations that day, I was drawn irrevocably into Chernobyl's eerie world.

Since then, I have travelled to the exclusion zone more than twenty times. Each journey has given me the sensation of returning to a sinister Narnia, as if to cross the zone's boundary is to pass through the wardrobe to another, phantasmagorical world. While the plant itself has continued to function, everything around it has been largely abandoned. Pripyat, a settlement to the northwest, where the plant's workers once lived, has become a ghost town, decorated with peeling Communist Party slogans and abandoned children's toys. On several occasions, as I wandered its deserted streets, a radio piped Soviet-era tangos from loudspeakers strung on the town's lampposts, as if inviting listeners to the last dance of the world. Beyond Pripyat, the zone's former villages seem under a terrible enchantment, now overgrown with plants and trees.

As the twentieth anniversary of the disaster approached, in 2006, I decided to revisit the contaminated zone one last time, hoping that I could put my insistent unease about Chernobyl to rest. The invisibility of the foe had proven difficult for me to photograph, just as it had been for the workers to combat. I decided also to seek out the "liquidators"—the men and women sent by the authorities to clean up the disaster's aftermath and build a sarcophagus to contain the toxic fourth reactor. Ever since, they have lived a troubled peace, veterans of a battle against an invisible enemy that only they can understand. Once everything had been made safe, their valour was quickly forgotten. Many of them became ravaged in later years, both physically and psychologically, and their faces mirror the poisoned land they left behind.

Precisely twenty years after the Chernobyl Atomic Power Plant caught fire, I found the families of firefighters who had battled the blaze seated by the graves of their loved ones. They, too, had come for closure, to mourn and say goodbye in a more formal way. They covered the graves with flowers and munched on open sandwiches with pickles, breaking their silence only to make the occasional toast to the dead.

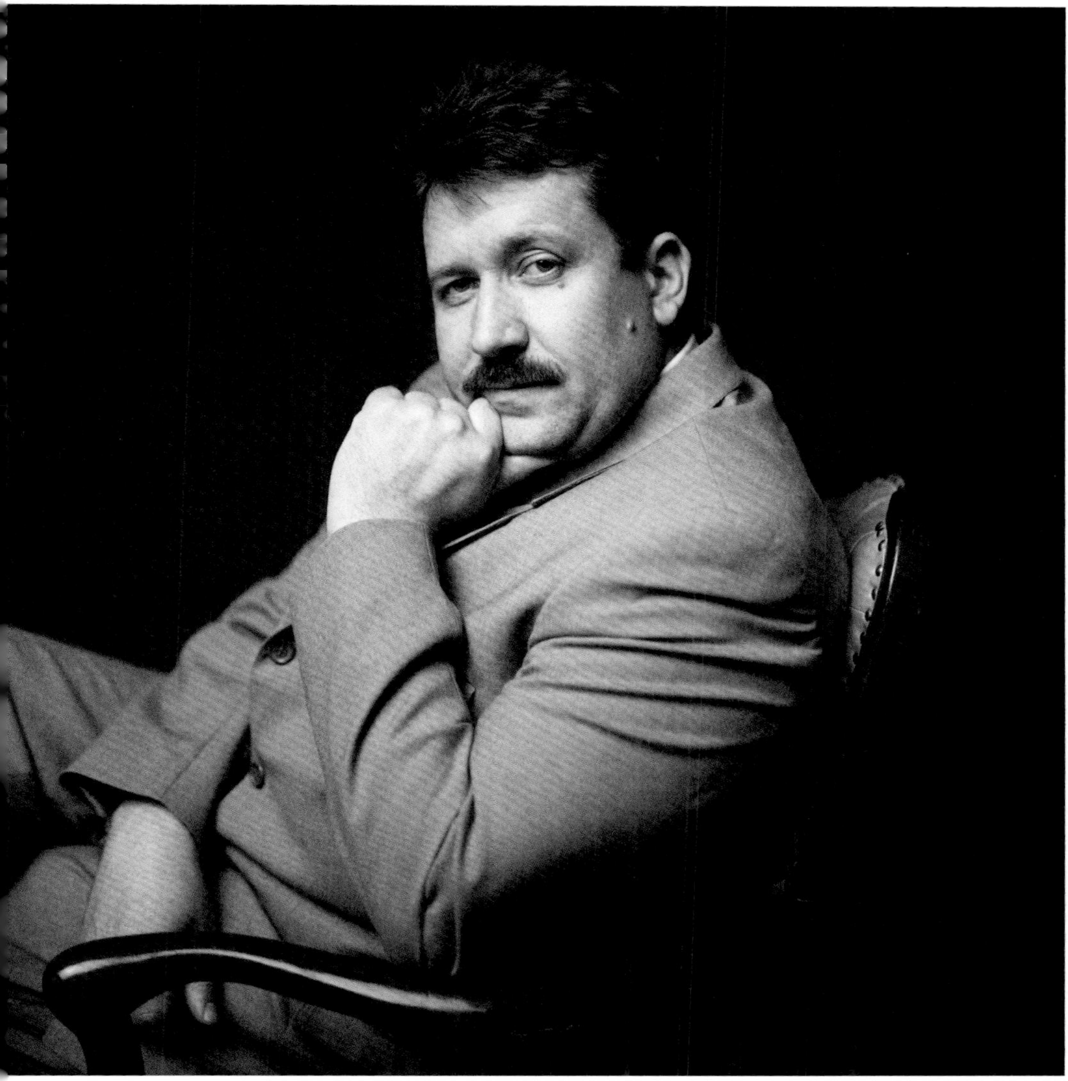

I was waiting for Viktor Bout on the pavement in front of a café when he and his brother pulled up in an electric-blue BMW 850 coupe with matching seats. Even though we were in Moscow rather than in one of the steamy capitals of tropical Africa he was known to frequent, Bout was wearing a pale-khaki safari suit. His brother, whose face was marked by a scar running diagonally down one cheek, wore the tired look of a bouncer who has had everything possible thrown at him. Bout took my hand within his enormous, unexpectedly soft grip and asked me to lead the way. His brother walked slightly behind us, carrying a spare suit.

Getting this alleged international arms dealer with an understandable aversion to publicity to agree to have his portrait taken for a cover story of *The New York Times Magazine* had been difficult. The only photograph of Bout in the public domain was one of him standing next to an Antonov cargo plane on a landing strip somewhere in Africa, dressed in slacks and a baseball cap.

I had first met Bout several weeks before, in a Moscow hotel lobby with two of his heavies and the journalist Peter Landesman. We drank coffee and chatted. Bout

Arms and the Man

Moscow
September 2006

spoke to us in good, if accented, English—he had once been a military trainer in Africa and was fluent in several languages—and he appeared eager to dismiss any preconceived impressions we might have held that he was a threat to world security. At one point, the conversation drifted to photography and, with a starry look in his eyes, he revealed that his deepest desire was to retire and become a wildlife photographer.

We met again for lunch a few days later, in an Azeri restaurant where we sat in a private room, concealed by a wall of multicoloured carpets. Afterwards, we walked onto the street to take some photographs. Although he had agreed to the interview, and therefore to sacrifice his precious privacy, the idea of being photographed was painful to him. He stood in front of me for less than a minute with a disgruntled look, as if to purposely confound me. I warned him that the portraits were not flattering, but he seemed not to care. As we walked on, I took Peter aside and asked him to persuade Bout to give me more time.

A week later, Peter called. Bout had finally agreed to another session, but it needed to be inside, somewhere hidden from view. A friend of mine ran a photo studio in central Moscow, and so we arranged to meet there.

I asked Bout to sit in an armchair that happened to be in the studio and started by photographing him with an old Rolleiflex, using a simple beauty lamp on one side. I worked fast and chatted with him to keep him distracted, fearing that at any minute he would simply get up and go. I didn't use a flash, because I thought it might irritate him, and as a result an unintentional imprecision, almost a sfumato effect, came over the portraits. Bout then decided to change suits. I photographed him with two strobe lights, which somehow made him look fiercer, less ambiguous. A few minutes later, his patience ran out and he abruptly walked away from the backdrop.

This image from the first set, in which he is looking at the camera with an almost fresh-faced regard, stood out. And yet the expression is impossible to define as being a smile, a smirk, or a threat. As we were saying goodbye, he paused. Looking me straight in the eye, he observed, with equal inscrutability, "If I don't like the pictures, the best thing that will happen to you is that I'll only break your cameras." And with that he was gone.

Although the notion of distance takes on an altogether different meaning in Russia, Chukotka remains beyond the pale. Waking in its capital, Anadyr, I was treated to the bewildering sight of watching the late-night news live from Moscow, nine time zones away. Even the gold mines of Magadan and the Kolyma peninsula, where tens of thousands of prisoners perished from cold and hunger in the most notorious of Soviet gulags, lie farther south, and the region is so inhospitable that it boasts five times as many reindeer as residents.

To live in Anadyr is, in itself, a statement of Russian bravado, a confrontation with the untamed frontier in the spirit of the Cossacks claiming Siberia, or Gagarin flying into the cosmos. Although the federal government steadfastly spends millions of dollars to maintain daily life in Chukotka, its vast swaths of tundra feel fit only for Eskimos and madmen.

I had come to Chukotka at the invitation of the World Wildlife Fund. The fund's Russian and American experts were meeting with indigenous Chukchi hunters to talk about polar bears. Since global warming began shrinking the polar ice pack and, with it, the bears' natural feeding area, polar bears had started scavenging local settlements for food. Despite the danger that this posed, the World Wildlife Fund wanted to encourage the hunters to scare the bears away rather than kill them.

Our destination was Vankarem, a hunters' village on the shore of the Sea of Okhotsk. We headed north from

Let Sleeping Dogs Lie

Vankarem, Chukotka
8 April 2007

Anadyr in two tracked vehicles, crossing fields blanketed by snow and navigating solely by GPS across the endless expanse of white towards our destination.

It was a three-day journey, and we slept on a mattress covering the width of the vehicle. The monotony—for it was almost impossible to see anything through the vehicle's tiny windows—was broken only by insistent rounds of vodka and sausage. At dawn on the second morning, the driver woke me to announce, with considerable excitement, that we were crossing the Arctic Circle. I stepped out to find a huge commemorative arch denoting the 66th parallel. Half buried in front of it was a sign marked "Diversion," which must have been a practical joke, for there was no road to be seen. Everything was buried under several feet of snow.

The hunters waiting for us at Vankarem had gathered from far across the region, and as soon as we arrived they set about filling us with local delicacies: whale-meat patties, smoked-walrus sausage, dried seal intestines. The next morning, the experts from the World Wildlife Fund began their speeches.

In Chukotka hunters were officially forbidden to shoot polar bears, except in self-defence. It was an open secret, however, that they killed them anyway, for their meat and their skins. Despite the wise words of the experts, the hunters closed their ears. Their way of life had not changed in decades and no one from Moscow, let alone from another continent, was about to change it now. The hunters sat nobly, silently, in their reindeer suits for three days, waiting for us to leave.

The last night of our stay the wind blew hard. I awoke at first light and walked through the village, stumbling upon a pack of sled dogs half buried by the snow. These dogs—known as Laikas, a Russian breed of husky—are not allowed inside, because they must never, even for a few minutes, become accustomed to the luxury of warmth.

Looking at the dogs, I saw survivors; like all those who roam the polar icecaps, whether man or beast, they share an existence that is constantly threatened and, because of that, is somehow heroic to me. At that moment, however, as the wind howled around me, I was struck by how snug the lead dog seemed under the snow, entirely blanketed but for a small space around the nose, where its breath had cut a narrow passage.

I took several rolls of film, admiring the dog's composure as my fingers became numb and the emulsion of the film creaked as I wound it, hardened by the bitter cold and threatening to snap at any moment.

When an elderly hunter arrived to rouse the dog and the rest of the pack, we exchanged the early-morning pleasantries of two men who had not intended to meet, falling back on the surest of topics, the weather. "It's warm today," he remarked—it was already a spring-like -28 degrees centigrade—as he quickly untied the dogs and marched them over to his sled, readying for his departure.

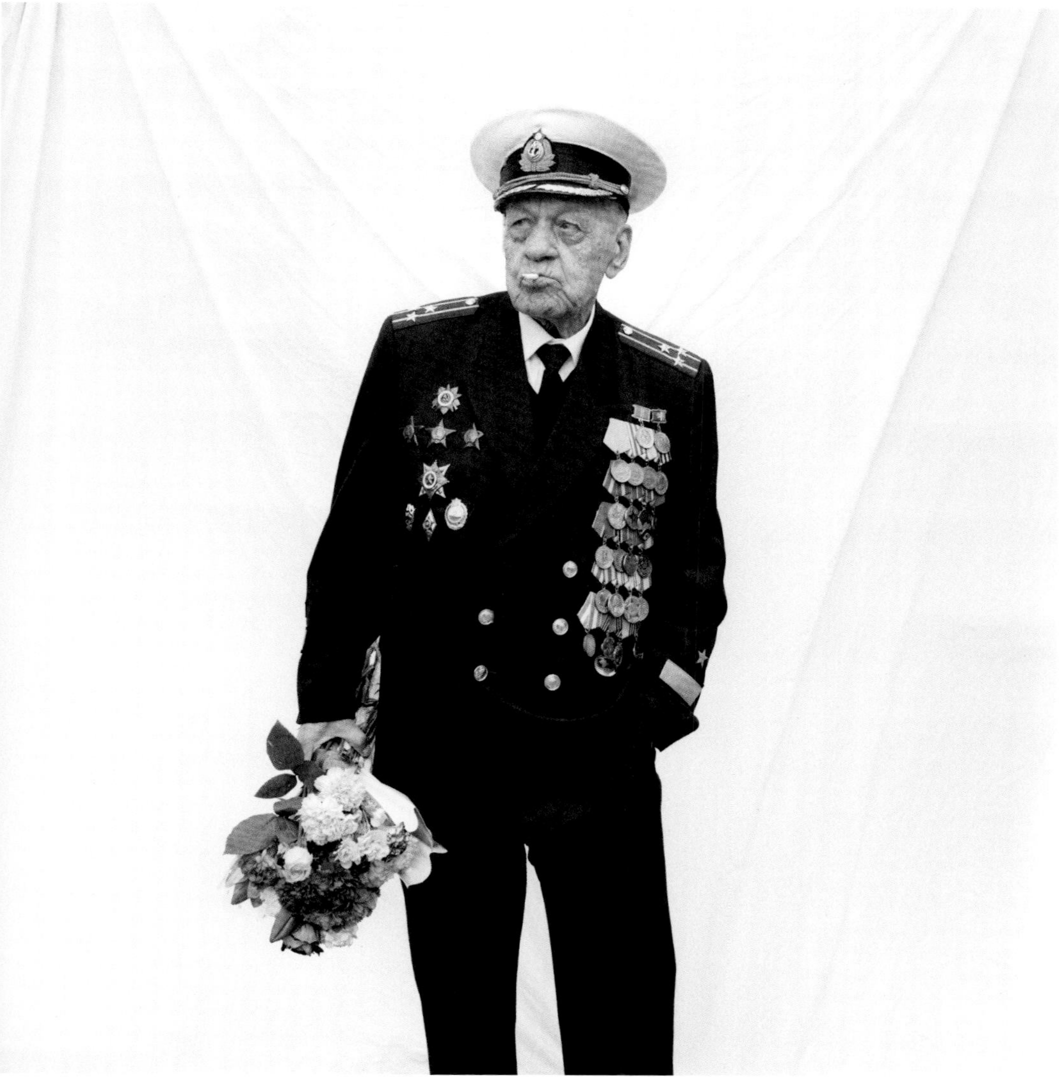

The Last Hero

Gorky Park, Moscow
9 May 2007

Yuri Stepanovich Zaguskin has always been my favourite. Of the hundreds of Russian World War Two veterans I have photographed, he remains for me the most charming.

In Russia, veterans of this war occupy a nostalgic and sacred pantheon. And ever since my first visit to Russia, I have watched them battling with age and—like anyone who has been to war—fighting with their memories as well.

Invariably, though, Soviet and Russian photographers posed the veterans in melodramatic guises, as if they were icons rather than individuals, heroes robbed of their identities. They bore little resemblance to the people I saw. Realising that their numbers were dwindling fast, I set off to find them on 9 May 2006 and then returned to photograph them for three successive years.

Victory Day, as 9 May is known in Russia, is an unbridled celebration of the defeat of Nazi Germany. Across the country, veterans dressed in their medal-clanking uniforms reunite. In Moscow, the most famous meeting place is Gorky Park, where they gather for a festive lunch of vodka, songs, and dances, which invariably ends with tears of one sort or another.

I waited for the veterans at the park's entrance, next to a makeshift studio I had furnished with a white backdrop. To entice them into letting me take their picture, and to thank them, I offered every one a Polaroid portrait to take home.

In the course of four years, I photographed more than five hundred veterans. Our meetings often became long and poignant, leaving me emotionally overwhelmed as I tried to navigate an endless stream of reminiscences. Sometimes those whom I had photographed on their way into the park would stop on their way out to give me a tearful farewell embrace, as if unsure of their return the following year.

Members of the public traditionally give flowers to the veterans, in gratitude for their valour and sacrifice, and Zaguskin, resplendent in his naval officer's uniform, had already collected a sizable bouquet by the time he entered the park. I asked him to stand in front of the backdrop, and he waited for me to take a picture. As I pressed the shutter, I found, to my exasperation, that I had come to the end of the roll in my Hasselblad. I told Zaguskin that I needed a minute to change the film, and he asked if there was time for a smoke.

When I had reloaded the camera, he was still puffing away. I took just one frame before he noticed that I was pointing the camera at him, whereupon he stubbed out the cigarette and returned his attention to the shoot. I finished the whole film, but that first image, in which he was looking off, lost in his thoughts, was far richer than the others. It was not a naval officer in front of me but an old matinée idol, caught unawares on the set.

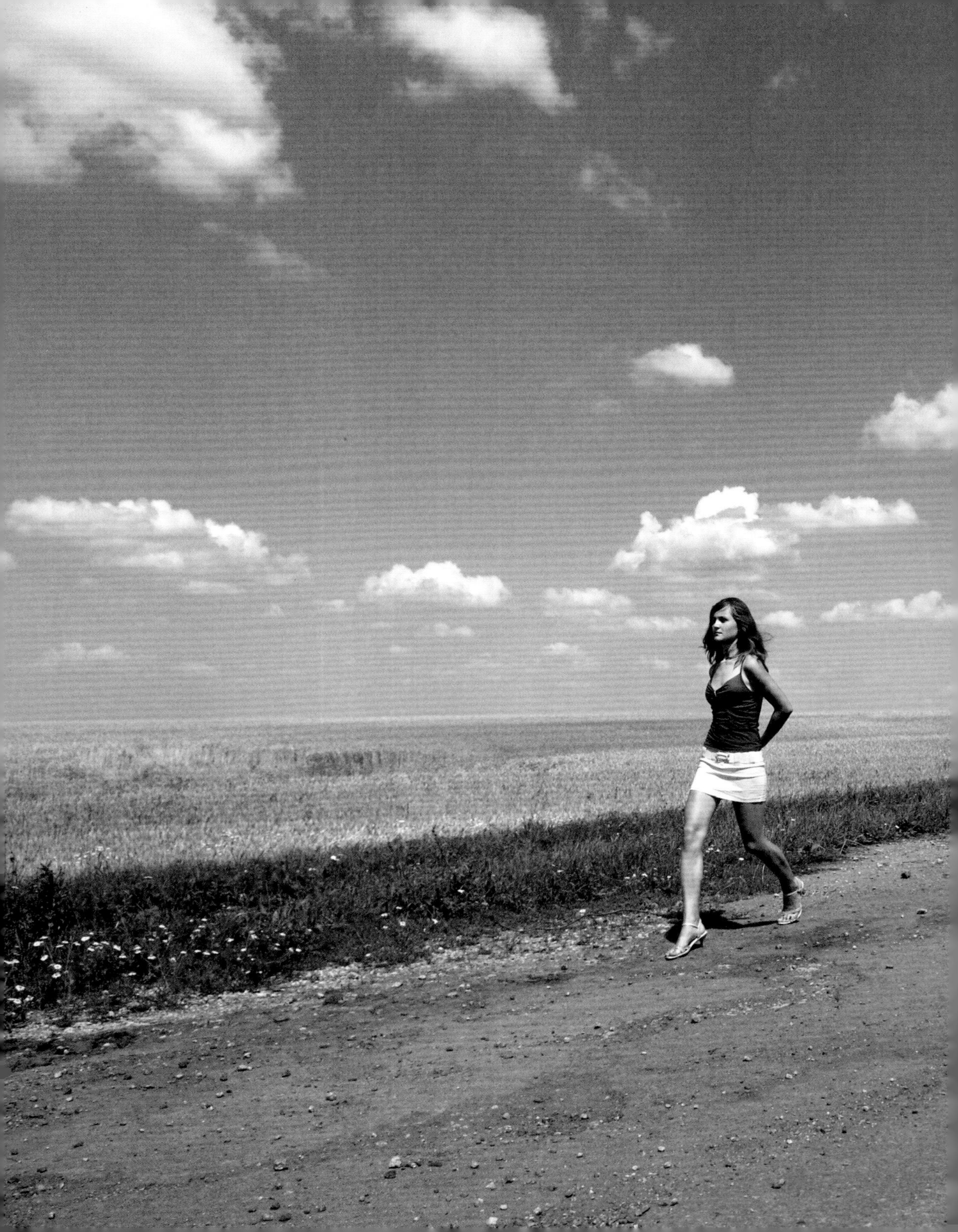

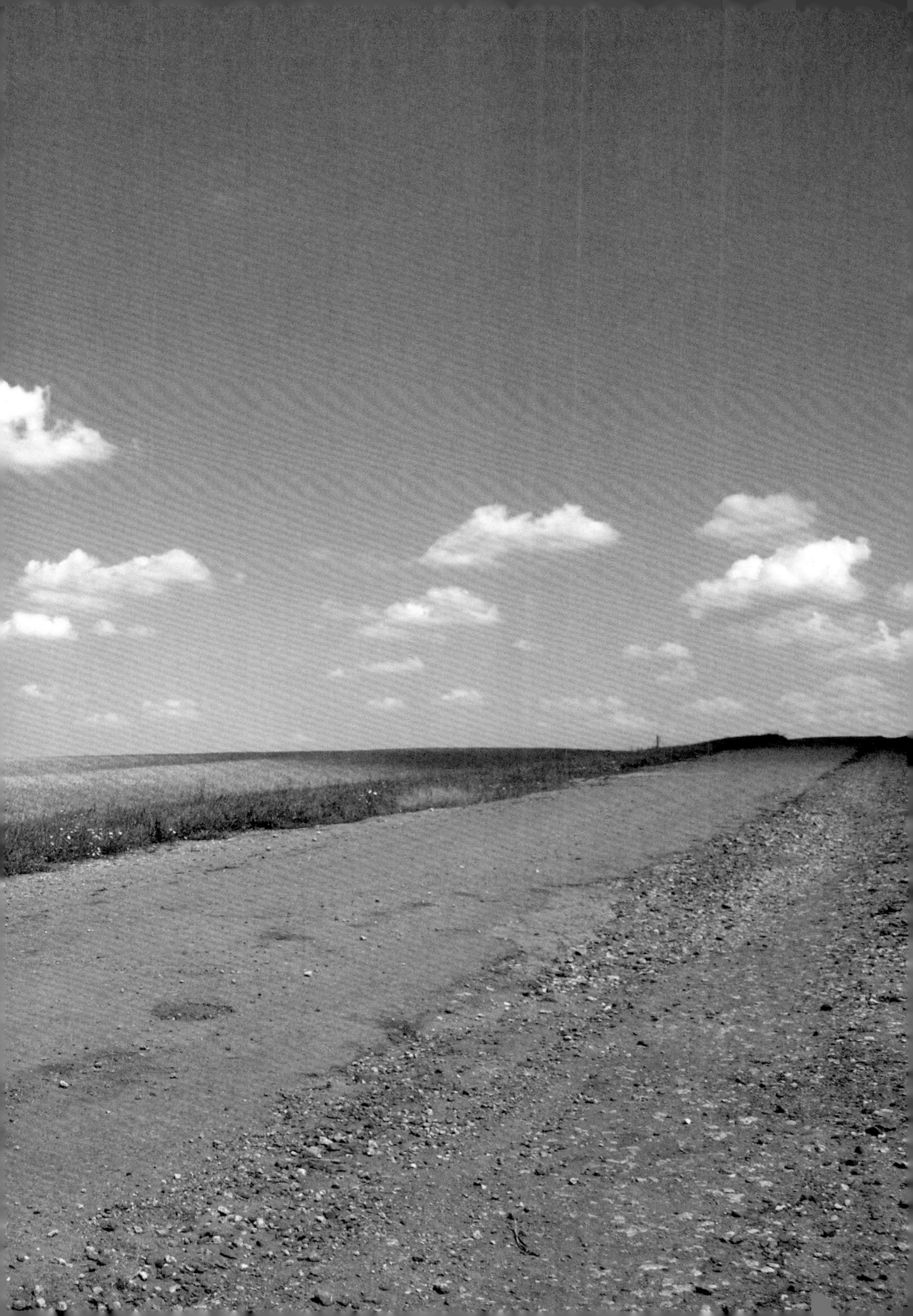

The Mirage

Lipetsk Region, Russia
14 July 2008

An assignment to photograph the upcoming harvest of Russia's largest landowner had promised a monotonous day; since the early morning, I had seen nothing but wheat stretched across the horizon. Searching in vain for something to focus on, I had stopped in the middle of the road to scan a field of cereal even more ridiculously large than the one I had photographed a half hour earlier when a figure on the horizon caught my eye: a girl striding towards me, presumably heading for the hamlet that I had just left behind.

Even from a distance, I could see that she carried neither a purse nor a shopping bag. Curious, I pulled over to the side of the road and waited for her to pass.

There was no one else in sight on that glorious summer day, and the only sounds were the rhythmic swish of wheat and the metallic click of her heels on the broken tarmac. She must have noticed me crouching by the side of the car with a large camera—it would have been difficult not to—but not a word was spoken between us and, like a proper heroine, she stared straight ahead.

As she walked briskly towards the hamlet, I drove on to see where she had come from. The road first crested a small hill and then met a two-lane highway, leading, it seemed, from nowhere to nowhere else. Whoever had dropped her off—a relative, a lover—was now long gone. Was she visiting, or coming home?

A sudden gust of wind caught the branches of the birch trees beside the road, interrupting my musings, and I returned my gaze with regret to the infinity of wheat all around me.

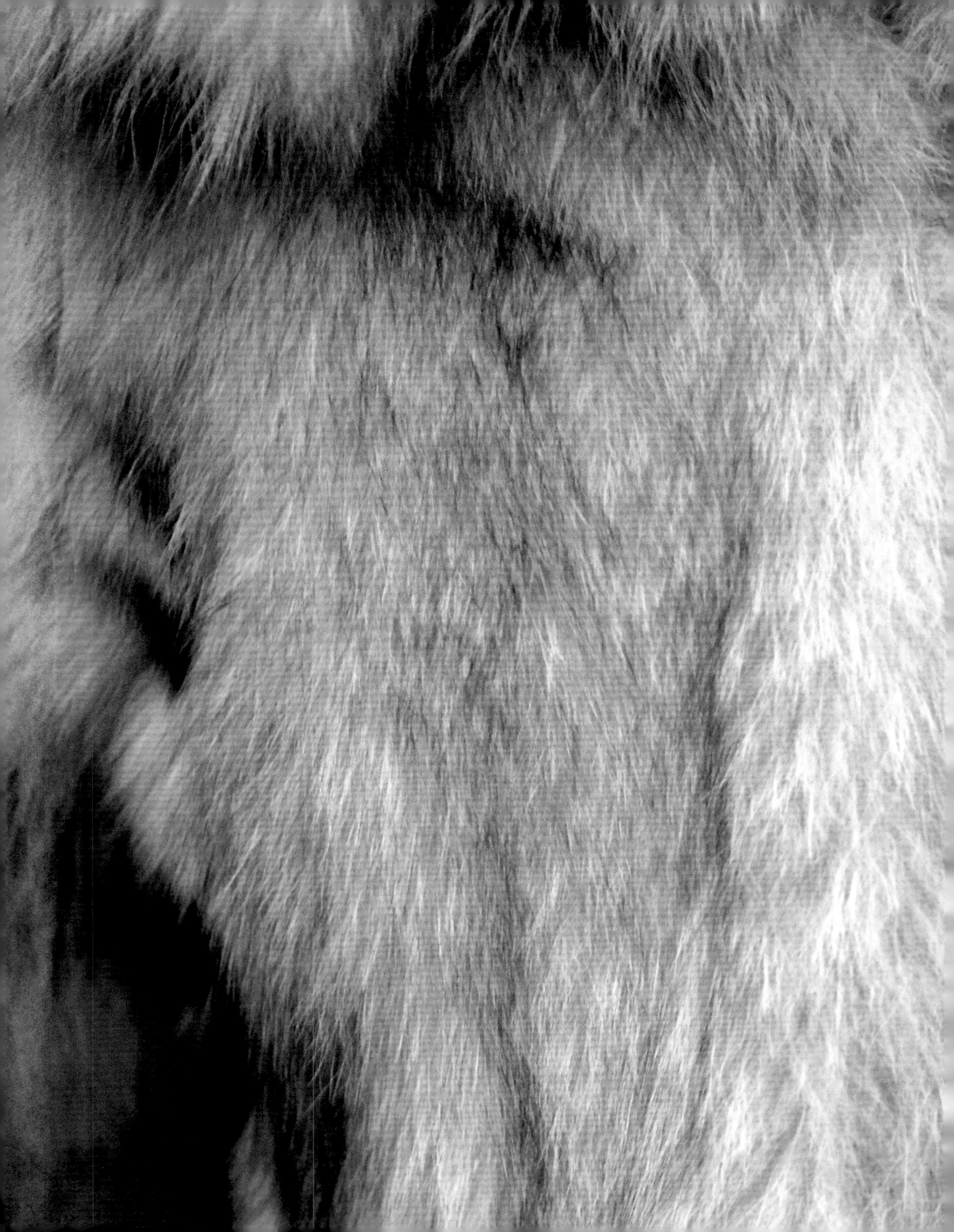

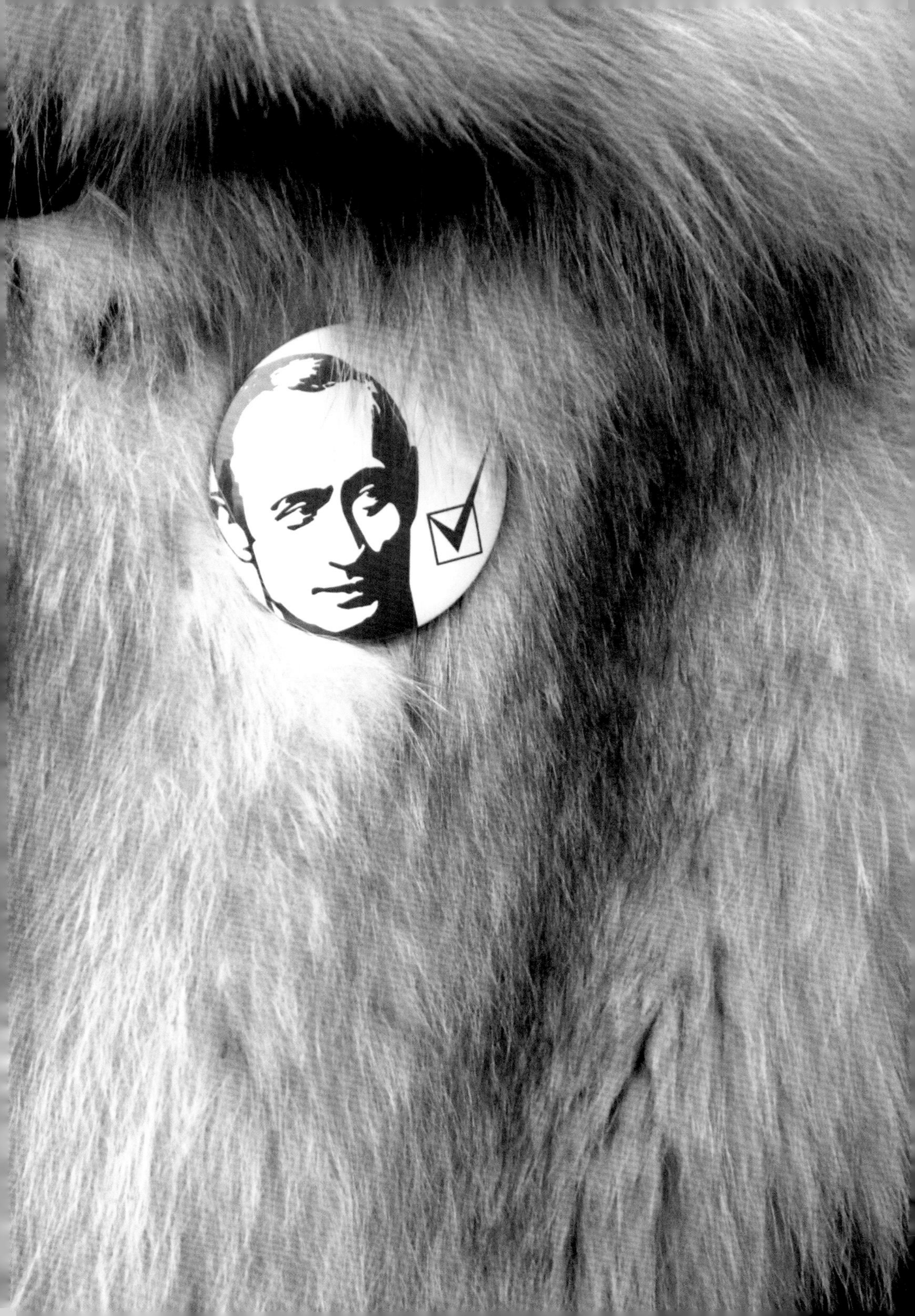

The Russian Bear

Nashi Demonstration, Moscow
24 November 2007

I have photographed Vladimir Putin dozens of times but never, to my regret, for an official portrait. Watching him at public events has been—as it is with politicians generally—an exercise in frustration, a search for texture in the polished exterior.

The relative intimacy and calm that surround an official portrait—even, sometimes, its awkwardness—can grant the photographer a glimpse of the person behind the personage. In large public gatherings, there is too much noise—not in an aural sense but in a visual one. Everyone is both guarded and distracted.

Even politicians who are not former secret agents, as Putin is, have grown increasingly comfortable maintaining a mask and narrowing the opportunities for candid images. Putin's press office, like the press offices of many state leaders, has sought to shape his image with carefully released pictures taken by its own photographers or those of the government-controlled agencies. In his roles as president and prime minister, Putin has been portrayed as a hunter-gatherer (fishing, his torso bared, in Siberia); a macho man (riding a Harley-Davidson); an archaeologist (bearing amphorae from the bottom of the sea); and a nature lover (guiding migratory cranes from an ultralight aircraft).

It is not surprising that world leaders are happy to be flattered; most of us are, too. But not all Soviet leaders have been so rigorous in controlling their image. Several years ago, I became a friend of Leonid Brezhnev's personal photographer, Vladimir Musaelyan, of Itar-Tass, who showed me a book of his years with the Communist General Secretary called "The Gensec and the Photographer." While many of Musaelyan's photographs burnish the former Soviet leader's image, others exhibit an astonishing openness in front of the camera. In one photograph, Brezhnev is answering a phone call at his dacha, a cigarette in his hand and his belly cascading over a pair of swimming trunks; in another, he is lounging in a track suit and slippers. Perhaps these images were meant for posterity, not for publication, but the fact that they were taken in the first place is, in itself, surprising: the political culture was known for eliminating fallen commissars and leaders from the public record with an airbrush.

Vladimir Putin has preferred, it seems, to personify Winston Churchill's mantra about Russia, and be "a riddle, wrapped in a mystery, inside an enigma." The Russian president is so rarely among the general public—he usually appears only on television and at official events—that he has also, in a certain way, become an icon, an image as real in a conceptual sense as in a physical one. When I saw this badge, pinned to the fur coat of a young student at a government-sponsored rally, I had the peculiar sensation that I was standing closer to Vladimir Putin than I ever had before—as if we were truly face to face and he were finally posing for that portrait.

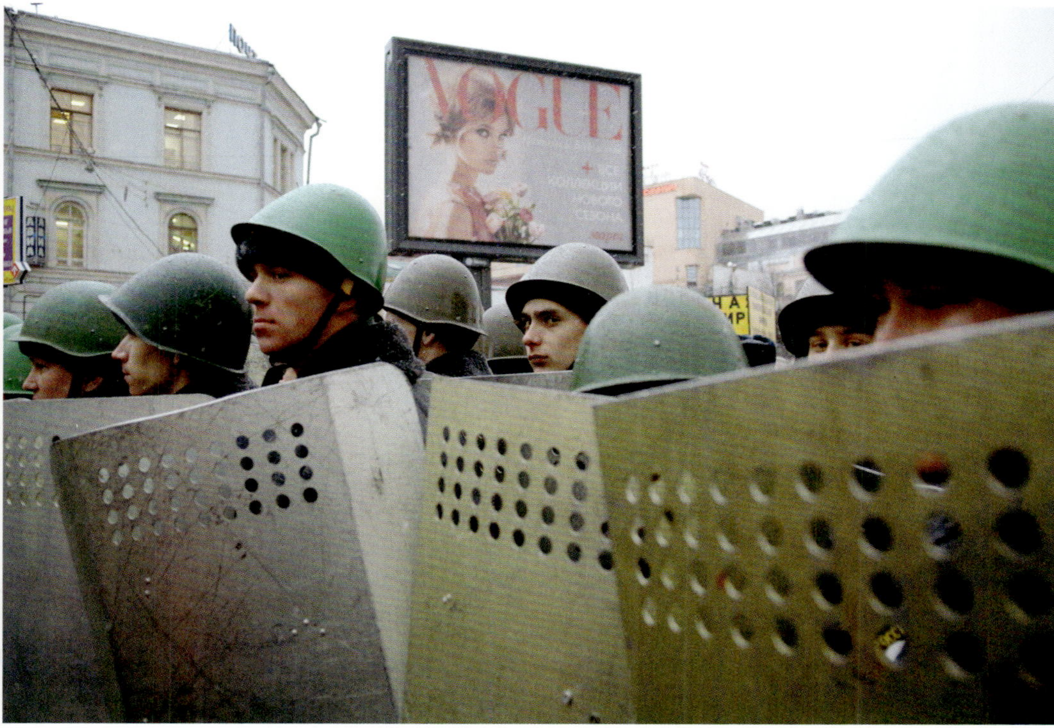
VOGUE
КОЛЛЕКЦИИ
НОВОГО
СЕЗОНА

Beauty and the Beast

Moscow
3 March 2008

It was the day after the Kremlin's candidate, Dmitri Medvedev, had predictably won the presidential elections, and I stood impatiently outside the Turgenev metro station with some journalists, Interior Ministry soldiers, and armour-clad riot police, awaiting the arrival of a group of protesters, the National Bolsheviks.

The Natsbols, as they were more commonly known, were an anarchical group led by the charismatic demagogue and writer Eduard Limonov. Their demonstrations, which were invariably illegal, had only one rule: be outrageous. Protesters would arrive at a location (usually the worst-kept secret in Moscow) and let off flares or smash something—anything to get themselves noticed and arrested. The riot police seemed to enjoy these theatrical encounters, which usually involved grabbing the demonstrators by any limb they could latch onto and throwing them into a nearby paddy wagon. The activists would be sentenced to a few days or a few weeks in prison and released; then they would repeat the process. The fact that barely a thousand people in all of Russia had ever been involved with the organisation did not dampen the protesters' enthusiasm, nor did it reduce the enormous show of force that was prepared each time to meet them.

Late-winter afternoons in Moscow have a particular sharpness. It is not a Siberian cold, which is simply bitter, but a humid one, which seeps into your bones. As I stood there shifting from one foot to the other, feeling distinctly chilled, I noticed the misery of the Interior Forces troops that were forming a human perimeter behind me, three men deep.

The soldiers had no doubt been standing in position for several hours, since many of them were shivering, their uniforms inadequate for the weather and their Soviet-era helmets barely fitting over their woolly hats.

Beyond them, a large billboard was rotating advertisements, one of them for *Vogue* magazine showing a summery portrait of a lovely Russian girl with a bunch of flowers. This incongruous meeting of two disparate Russias—the beautiful and the brutal—seemed far more intriguing than the encounter with the third, dissident Russia that I was awaiting. Often the unexpected show in the wings provides a more memorable image than the main performance does. And so it proved.

Half an hour later, the protesters, about twenty in all, came to set off some flares and shout "Death to the regime." They were duly arrested. The soldiers wheeled around and marched off to the empty trucks that awaited them. And the pretty girl kept on turning.

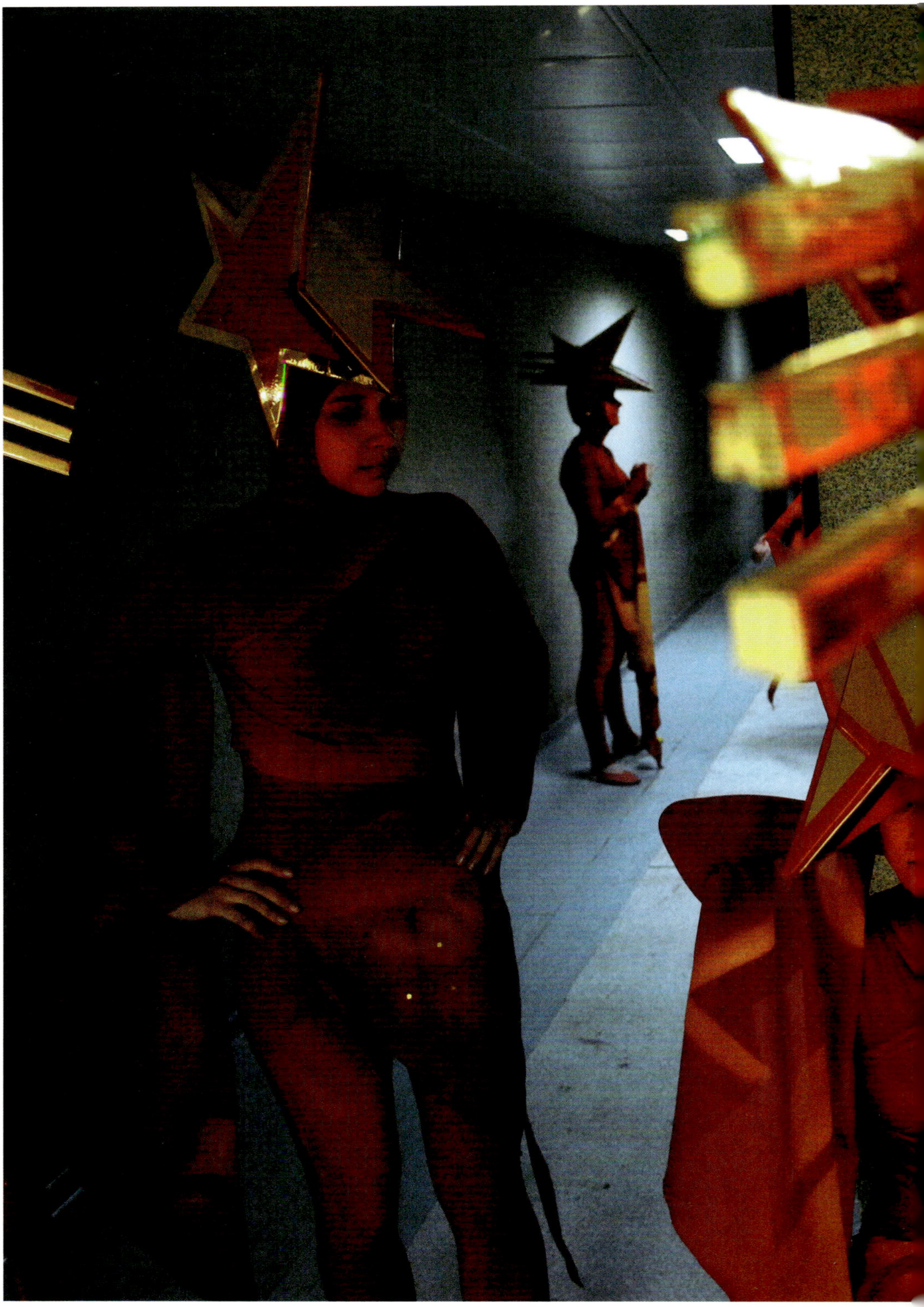

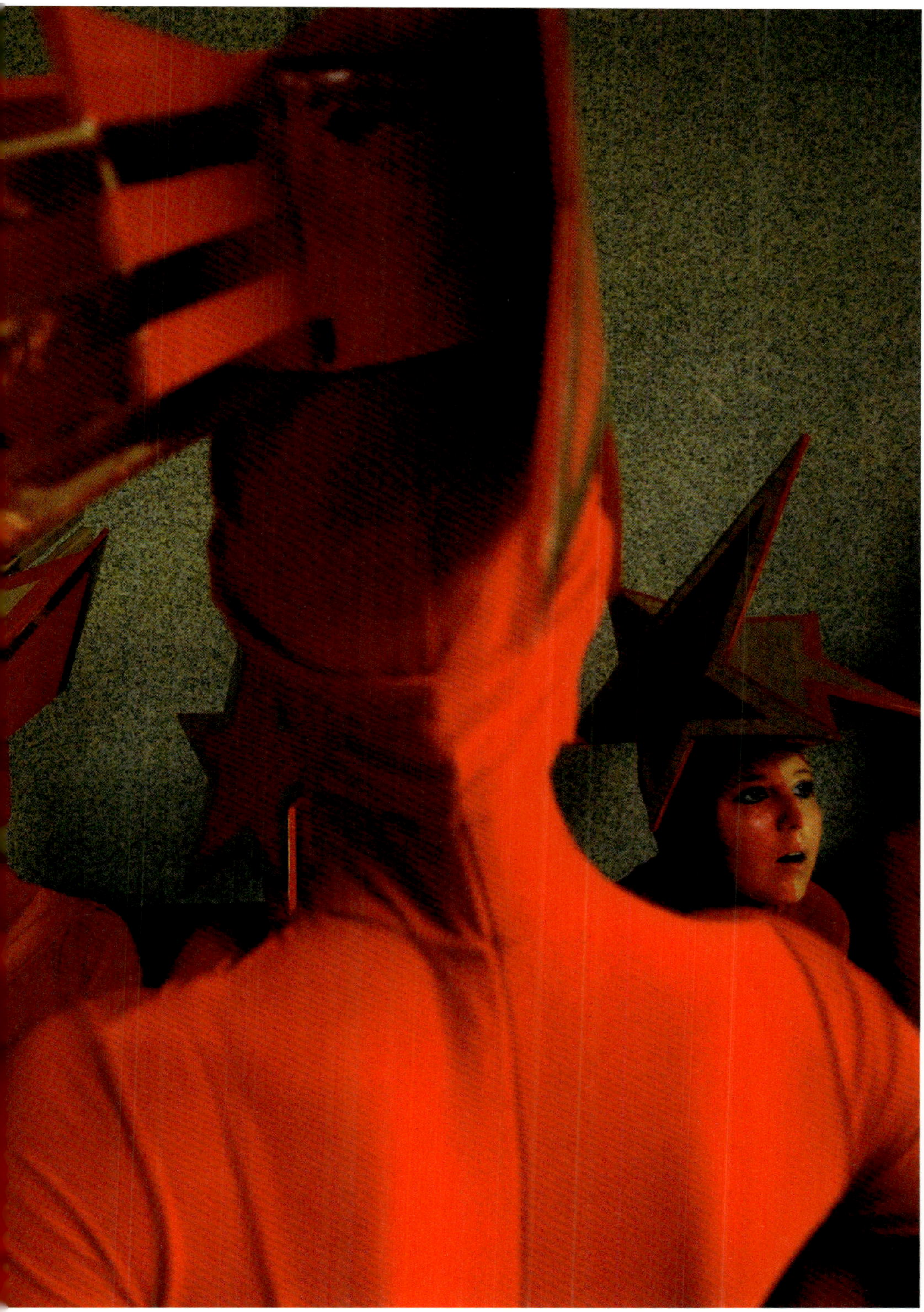

Champions

Luzhniki Stadium, Moscow
21 May 2008

When the Champions League final between Chelsea and Manchester United came to Moscow in 2008, I hurriedly found myself an assignment, although I was an imposter. On the accreditation form it would have been more accurate to have described myself as a Chelsea supporter than as a sports photographer. When Ronaldo opened the scoring with a beautiful header in the twenty-sixth minute, I was too busy admiring his perfectly timed jump to fire the shutter at the exact moment, instead doing so a split second later. I was also still thinking about the performers for the pre-game show, whom I had met by the tunnel entrance to the stadium before the kick-off.

Perhaps Moscow has always been awash in pretty girls, but since the end of the Soviet Union tales about them have taken on the proportions of an urban myth. When I moved from Moscow to Rome, at the end of the 1990s, I was invariably asked by Italian men at cocktail parties whether the rumours about statuesque blondes standing on every Moscow corner were true. I would pause for effect before answering, "Yes," and watch their mental departure from the glories of the *seicento* palazzo in which we were standing to the streets of the Russian capital.

It is not just their beauty that astonishes me but their lack of fear. Only Russian women, I believe, could have worn these uniforms—which a functionary must have dug out of some basement filled with leftovers from the 1980 Olympics—with such confidence.

Those enormous stars, somewhat ridiculous and seemingly out of scale for the heads they adorned, harked back to a Soviet era long before that of the Moscow Games. I imagined these young women waiting to take part in a parade on Red Square in the 1930s, when it was regularly flooded with youth holding athletic poses and oversized slogans of Agitprop. I pictured Alexander Rodchenko—the doyen of Russian avant-garde photographers, whose work, like that of all the great photographers, has shaped our visual language—tilting his Leica ever so slightly at some futuristic angle while Stalin looked sternly on from Lenin's tomb at the glittering smiles of the crowd below.

As the performers chatted, the sound of some eighty thousand football fans, loud and mostly British, rumbled through the corridors above and around us. But it seemed to have little, if any, effect on the performers' nerves. A few minutes later, I saw them on the pitch, dancing and swirling, smiles glued to their faces, before they disappeared back into the tunnel and the depths of the cavernous stadium.

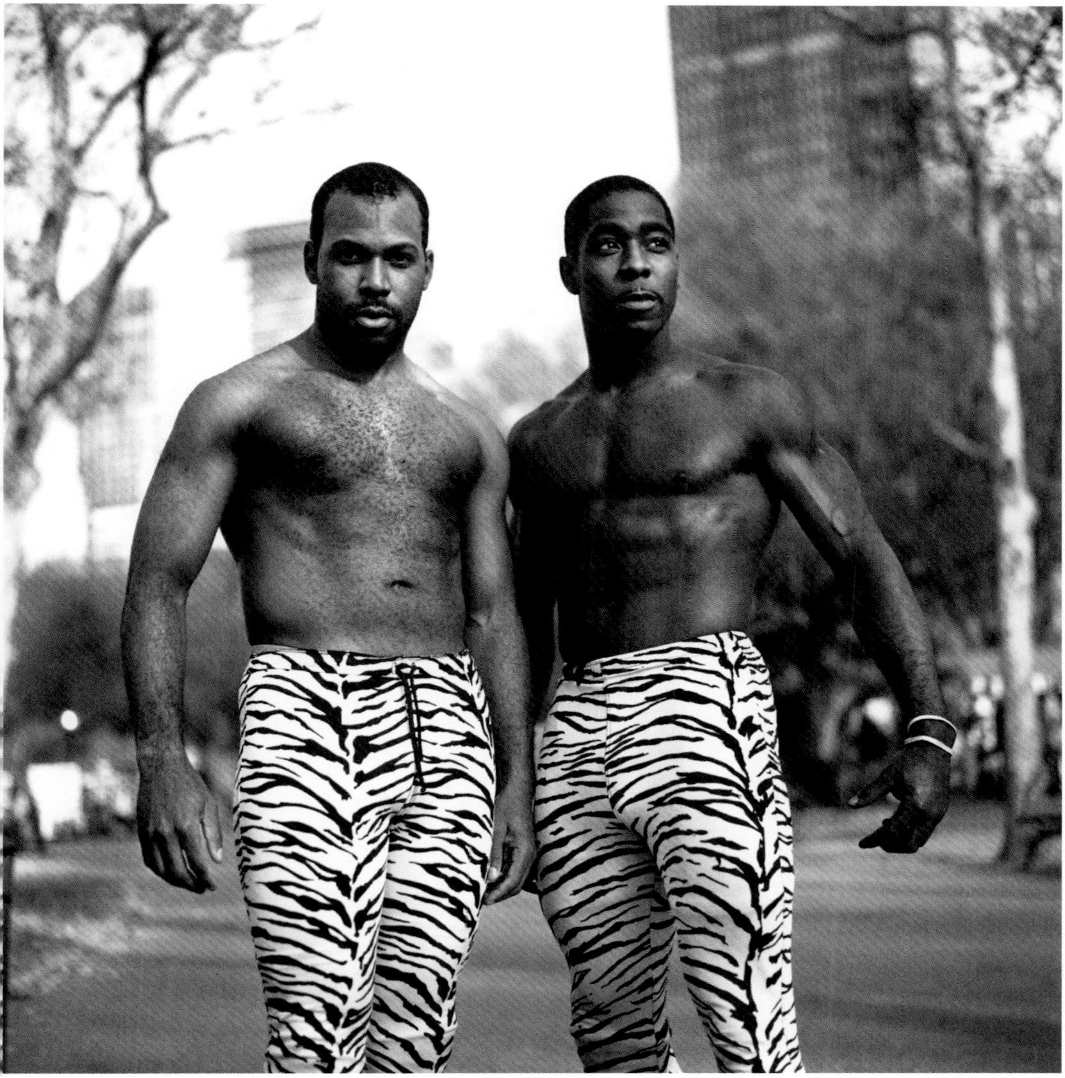

The Positive Brothers

New York
12 November 2008

Like many visitors to New York, I feel familiar with it—not simply because I have been there but because the thousands of images I've seen of it on television and in films have become part of my kaleidoscopic impressions of the city.

When I was invited by *The New York Times* to create a photographic portrait of this metropolis as seen through the eyes of a foreigner, I often felt caught between these existing and imaginary worlds. Whether I was photographing in Manhattan, Brooklyn, or the Bronx, it was impossible to escape the sense that I had seen it all before in someone else's movie—or even in my own dreams.

One afternoon, while aimlessly riding the subway, I decided to get out at Wall Street. At first, everyone seemed to be playing his proper part: the two beefy policemen directing traffic; a group of Fordham Business School students dressed like wannabe millionaires, in spiffy dark suits with white pocket handkerchiefs. Then I wandered into Battery Park, at the foot of Manhattan, where the Positive Brothers—a.k.a. Khrist Newman and Alphonso Stewart—were performing an acrobatic routine for a small crowd of onlookers and tourists.

It was a cold day to be wearing little more than a pair of stretch zebra leggings and gym shoes, and they threw themselves furiously into the routine, shouting "HEY!" as often and as loudly as they could, as if to warm their torsos. They tumbled and flick-flacked and even somersaulted over a few reluctant volunteers pulled from the audience while city folk all around us continued to make their unhurried way to the waterfront, bypassing our little island of intensity.

After ten minutes, the two acrobats wrapped up the show, every trick revealed, circling the spectators with an upturned cowboy hat in the hope of attracting a few dollar bills. The crowd melted away at their approach, leaving the Positive Brothers to transfer their slender earnings into a rucksack. Standing alone at the end of a day's work, they paused for some photographs before picking up their boom box and heading to the subway: fellow travellers, drifting between fantasy and reality.

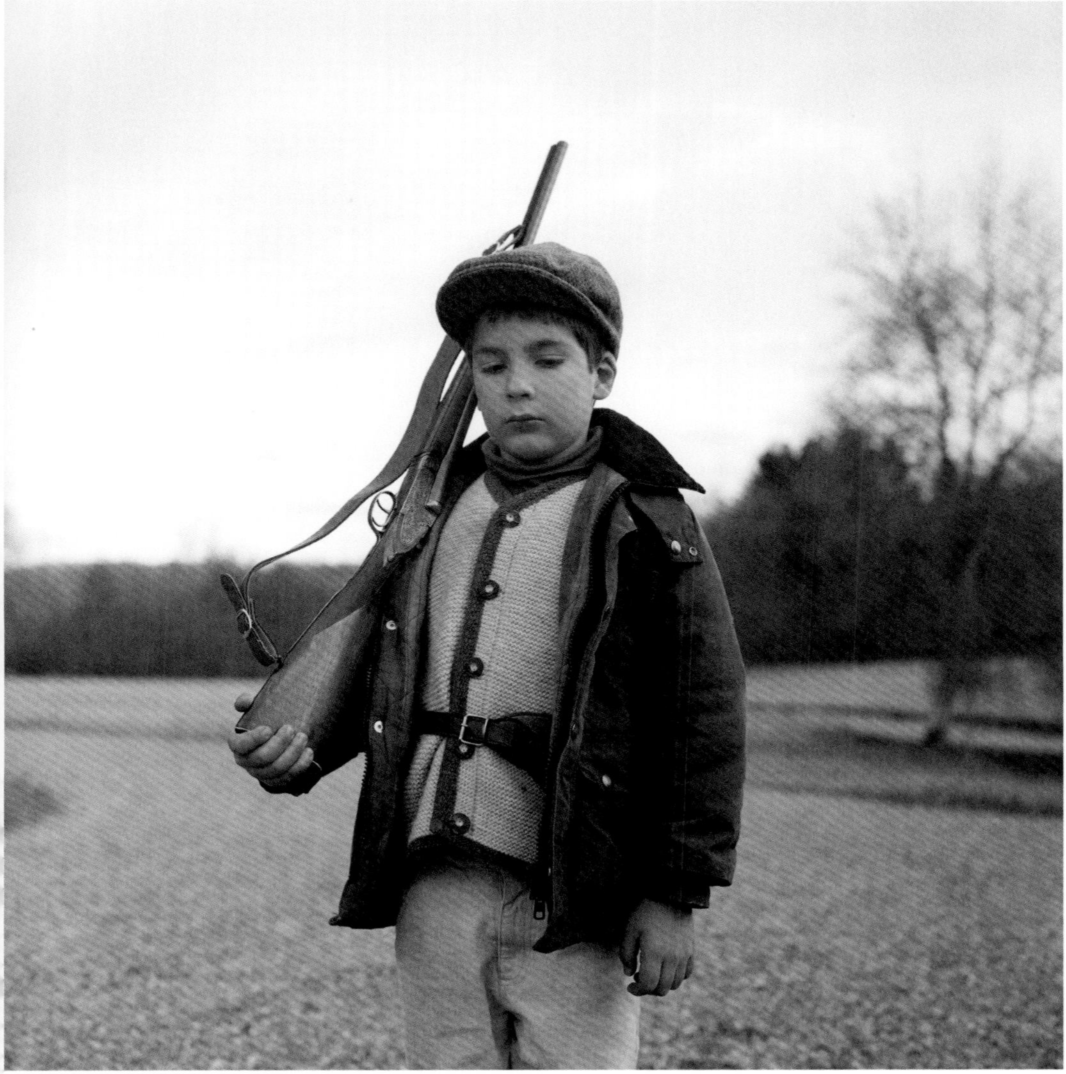

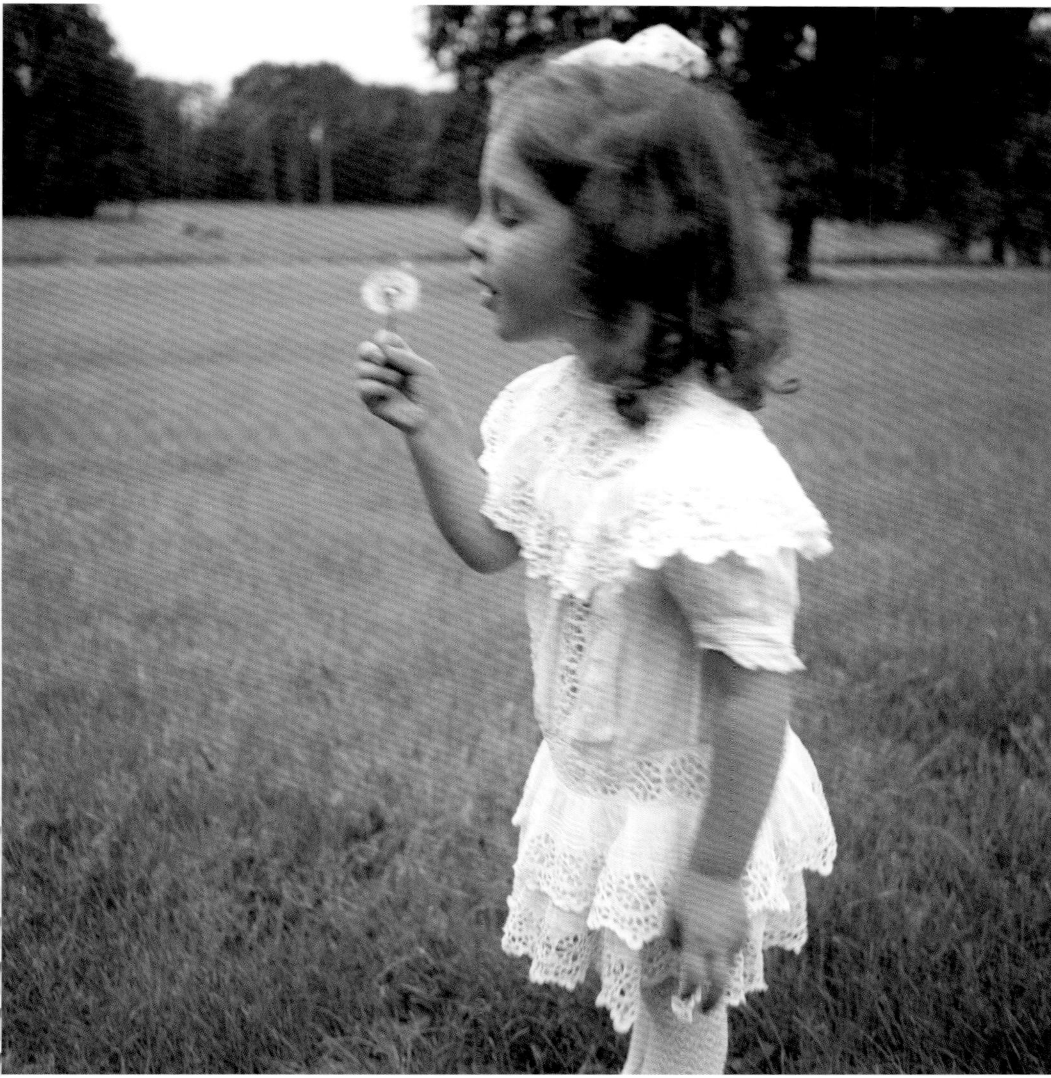

The Angels

Maillebois, France

2007

As a father and a photographer, I have the impression of seeing my children's lives as a perpetual series of moments—each one, no matter how slight, with its own weight and value. And like a juggler nervously lifting his gaze to a sky filled with objects to catch, I worry about how many of those moments will inevitably slip through my fingers.

I rarely ask my children to pose for me. The images are emotional rather than aesthetic, filled with a parent's affection and its complications. Seeing my own imprecise reflection in their faces, I sometimes sense unconscious hints of the detachment that will surely come. If I have enjoyed their company with an unquestioned proximity—always a photographic luxury—it is with the knowledge that, in time, a certain distance will be required.

I cherish the intimacy of these photographs but find it hard to judge them. Photographing my children is more complicated than I like to admit, since it is not only a question of capturing their lives but, equally, of fixing them to my own. My emotional compass is remagnetised by their presence, straightened each time to point true.

Not that my children believe that our closeness renders these images more truthful. They usually claim that my portraits bear only the slightest resemblance to themselves—or, at least, to their perception of themselves. A child of almost any age surely imagines that a parent can never hope to understand him or her. So in the end these photographs become simple celebrations of my children's childhood—a way to prove to myself that, despite so many days spent far away, I was there, too. And years from now, long after these photographs were taken, my children will be able to look at them and understand that as well.

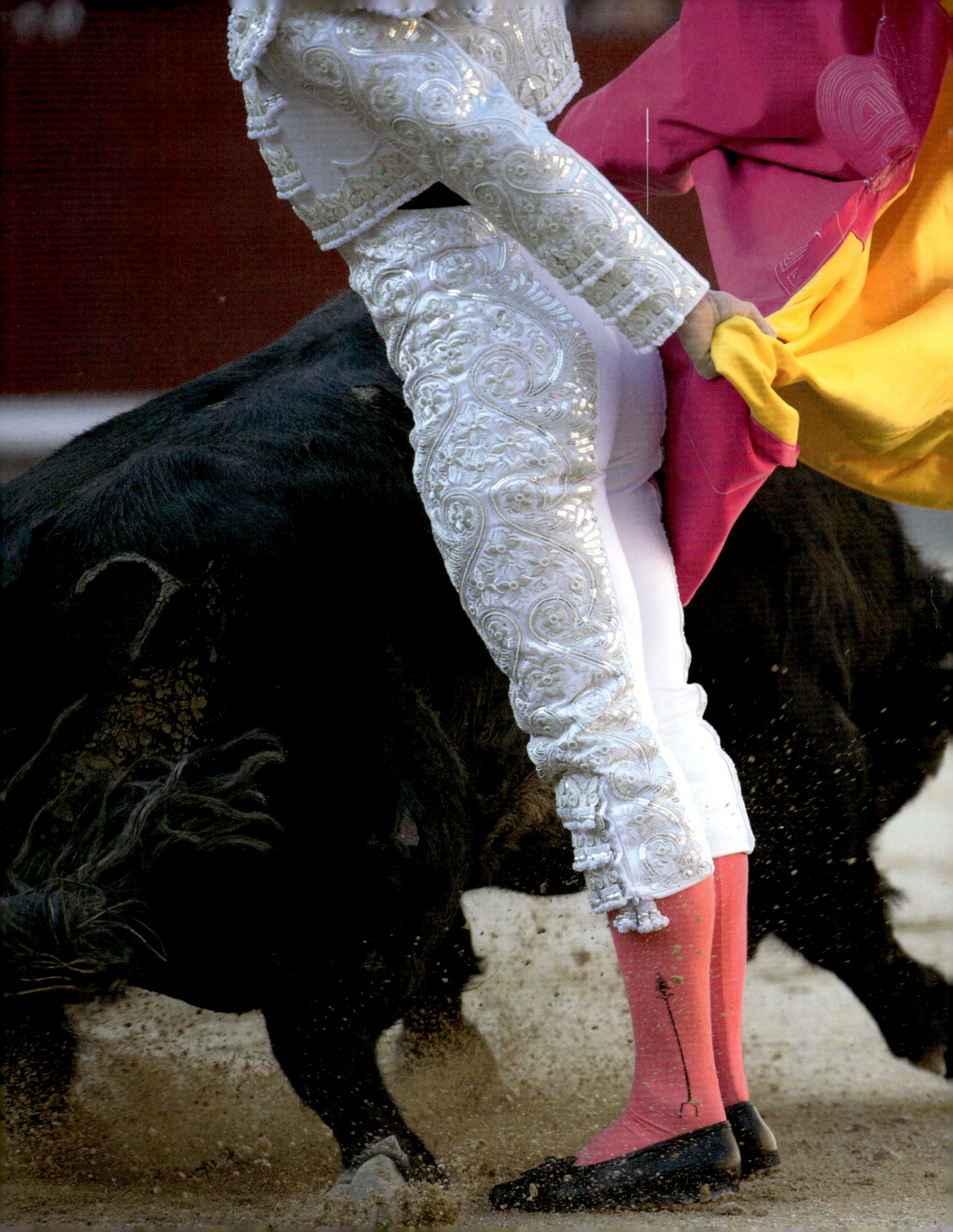

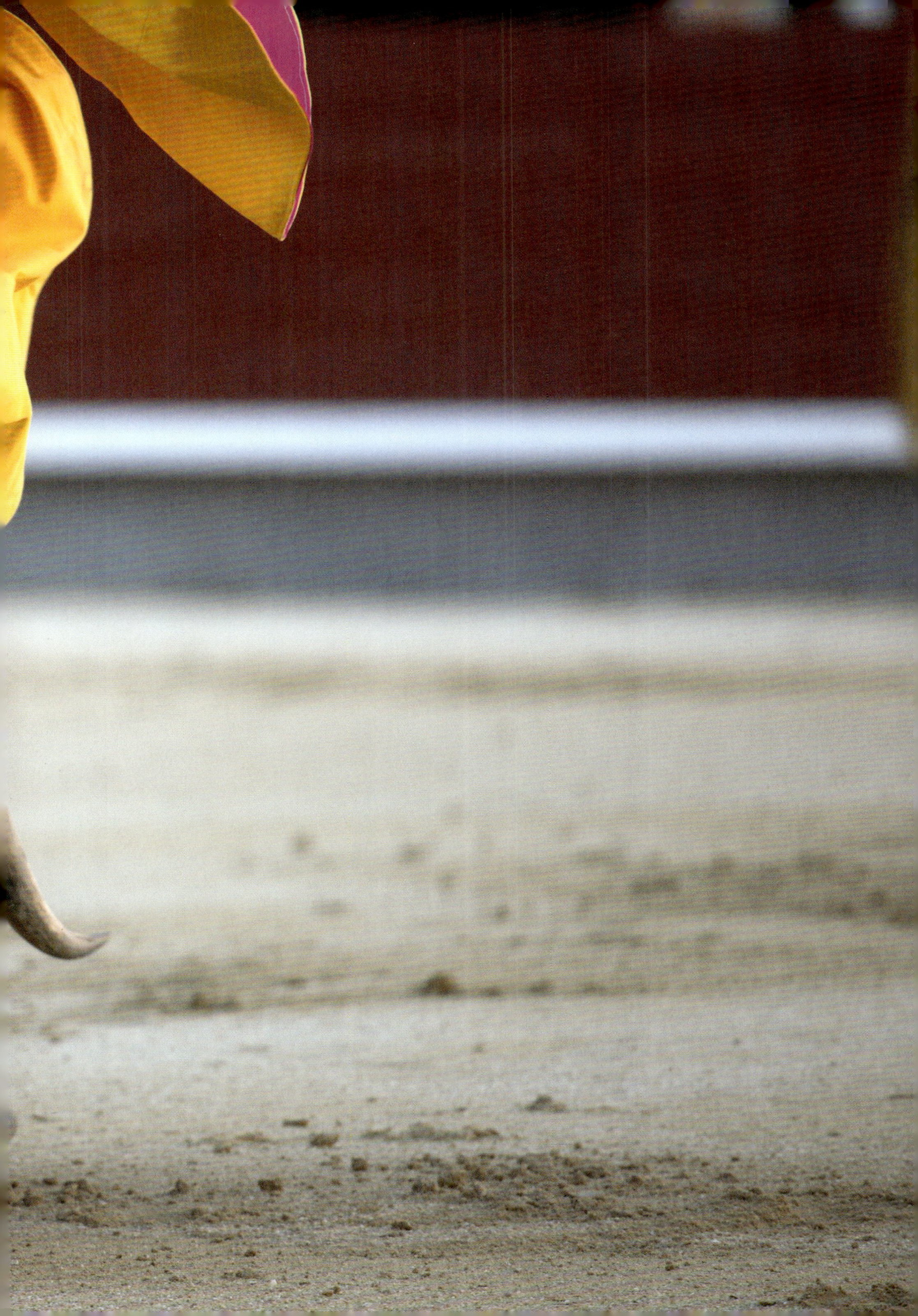

I know that you should never take to heart anything someone says to you at a dinner party. But in the winter of 2009, when the Spanish songwriter José María Cano told me that I couldn't be a real photographer because I had never photographed a bullfight, my pride was hurt.

A few months later, I chanced upon the Spanish Embassy's cultural attaché in Moscow, who was sifting through proposals for the upcoming Year of Spain and Russia. I cheekily suggested that he commission a project on bullfighting. I called him constantly and pestered him with emails to persuade him of my commitment. Finally, he agreed, his only fear being the possible ridicule he would receive at the Ministry for sending an Englishman to Spain to photograph bullfighting.

I understood his reluctance. Apart from reading Hemingway's *Death in the Afternoon,* I knew very little about tauromachy. I therefore proceeded to ask every Spaniard I could find for ideas of places to see bullfighting or the names of bullfighters to follow. I heard passionate and deeply entrenched beliefs either demonizing or revering bullfighting, but nobody could agree on where the best corrida in Spain was to be found.

In the end, I decided to concentrate my story around Madrid's famous three-week celebration of bullfighting, the Festival of San Isidro.

Nights of San Isidro

Las Ventas, Madrid
16 May 2010

During the day, I passed hours with former bullfighters, breeders, tailors, and teachers, to immerse myself in their world. And each evening I returned to Las Ventas, the city's historic bullring, to watch the six corridas scheduled for that particular night.

Strangely, the violence did not shock me, perhaps because I had seen far worse, albeit of a different kind. And although drawn to the aesthetic of the corrida—the peculiar union of its two opposing forces, brutality and beauty—I found myself increasingly fascinated by the psychological spectacle. When I looked at the ring, I saw two beings utterly alone, despite being surrounded by twenty-four thousand people.

Solitude seemed common to nearly all the bullfighters I met. Luis Bolivar, the Colombian toreador, allowed me into his hotel room as he prepared for the evening's corrida. Yet after a minute I was invisible to him. He squeezed into his tights and costume as I stood barely two metres away, as oblivious of my presence as he was of the scars scattered across his body.

As I watched the matadors stand in the tunnel before entering the ring for the *paseíllo*, they appeared distant, contemplative, their faces reflecting both confidence in their art and a sense of their own fragility. They were perfectly aware of the line they were about to cross, from the safety barrier into a space bereft of forgiveness—both for the bull and for themselves. Even if their swords wielded the power of life and death, they were not alone in dictating the outcome of the next few hours.

It was Juan Belmonte, considered by many the greatest of bullfighters, who in the early twentieth century pioneered standing close to the bulls. His legs were deformed; unable to leap from harm's way like other matadors, he instead stood still and made the bull run around him, thereby inventing this radical flirtation with danger. He received twenty-four serious injuries and countless minor ones, retiring several times and then returning to the ring. Then, just before his seventieth birthday, he shot himself rather than face illness and old age.

Every bullfighter, even the great ones, knows that he will be injured, if not killed. Yet few have relinquished the allure of the fight in their prime. One night at Las Ventas, a young French matador, Sebastián Castella, left the arena with his head bowed, as if weighed down by the moment just before, when he had killed his second bull of the evening. He limped slightly, and his torn and bloody trousers exposed a wound where the bull had caught him at the end of the *faena*. Yet his cut would soon be stitched, and in a few nights he would return to the ring.

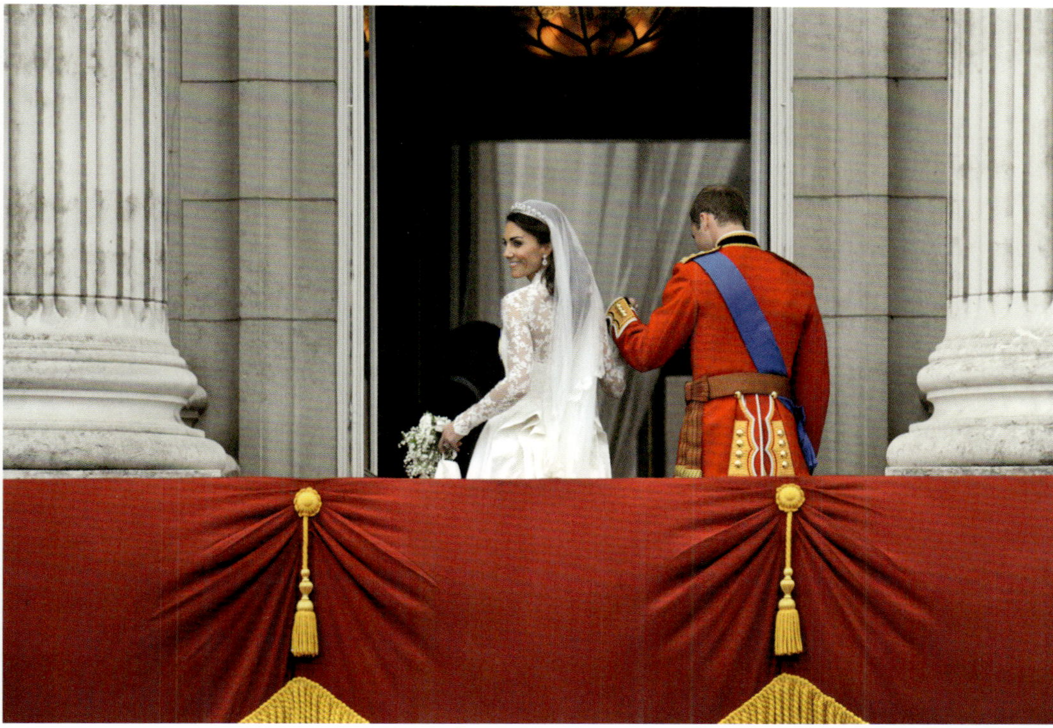

I arrived outside Buckingham Palace at 5:30 a.m. sharp. As an Englishman, I would have felt terrible arriving late for the royal wedding. Besides, I was already far from alone.

The Mall outside the palace brimmed with brightly dressed folk, many of whom had camped there overnight. Giggly girls in fake tiaras clutched bottles of champagne, boys stood about naked but for their Union Jack shorts, and grandmothers in coloured deck chairs poured extra-strong cups of tea, beaming at all and sundry.

After showing my credentials to the police, I crossed the security line towards the photographers' stand, at the front of the Queen Victoria Memorial, opposite the palace. The stand consisted of four rows, each holding sixteen places. Every spot had a direct view of the palace's balcony and had cost £900 to purchase.

I clambered to my position, No. 43, in the third row, somewhat right of centre, where I was sandwiched between photographers from *The Sunday Mirror* and *Time* magazine. It was quite a feat to squeeze myself, my cameras, two enormous telephoto lenses, a tripod, and—this being England—two umbrellas into my

The Royal Wedding

London
29 April 2011

allotted space, which had been clearly delineated by thick lines of red tape. The result felt somewhat akin to sitting in a very expensive open sardine tin.

When the newly wed Charles and Diana had kissed on this same balcony, thirty years earlier, the public royal embrace had marked an extraordinary break from protocol. In addition, a now famous photograph had caught the exact moment their lips met—making the kiss appear deeply passionate when it was in fact nothing more than a quick peck that caught Charles by surprise. On this particular morning, the balcony looked very much farther away to me than it had the day before, and I wondered how, at this distance, it would be possible to make a photograph that differed from anyone else's.

I sat down and waited, chatting with my neighbours as we shared coffee and digestive biscuits. At 9 a.m., we saw the first stirrings of activity across the road when stewards stepped onto the balcony to appoint it with the traditional swagged and fringed drape. Then a cleaning lady came to vacuum it. At 10 a.m., members of the royal family departed from the palace for the wedding ceremony, at Westminster Abbey. Finally, shortly after midday, we had our first glimpse of the newlyweds as they arrived in an open carriage and drove through the gates of Buckingham Palace.

At 1:25 p.m., eight hours after I had arrived, William and Kate stepped onto the balcony. It was the moment that the world—and the sixty-four photographers on the stand—had been waiting for. The royal couple kissed, and the sound of camera motor drives whirred all around.

A bit later, they kissed again, and we all fired away with our cameras a second time, grateful for another embrace. The crowd, too, greeted each kiss with a roar of approval and shouted for more. But a copy is rarely better than the original, and the crowd sensed that as well. With Kate and William, the interesting moment came at the end.

The Prince, cool and poised, turned to lead his bride inside. Just before stepping into the palace, though, the Duchess turned around for one last glimpse of the vast crowd stretched down the Mall. It was as if she wanted to reassure both herself and her audience that it wasn't, in fact, a dream—that perhaps one truly could marry a prince and live happily ever after.

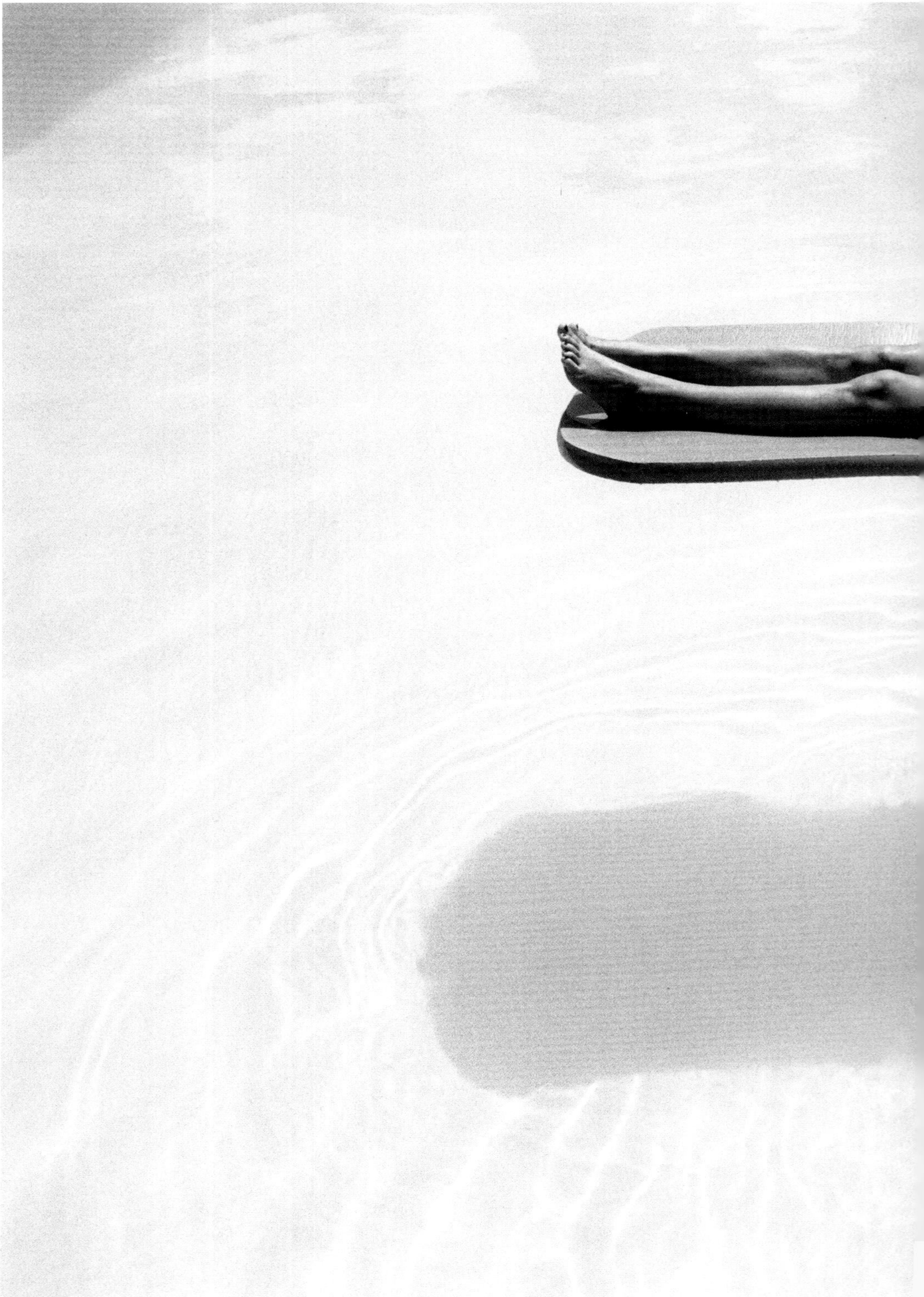

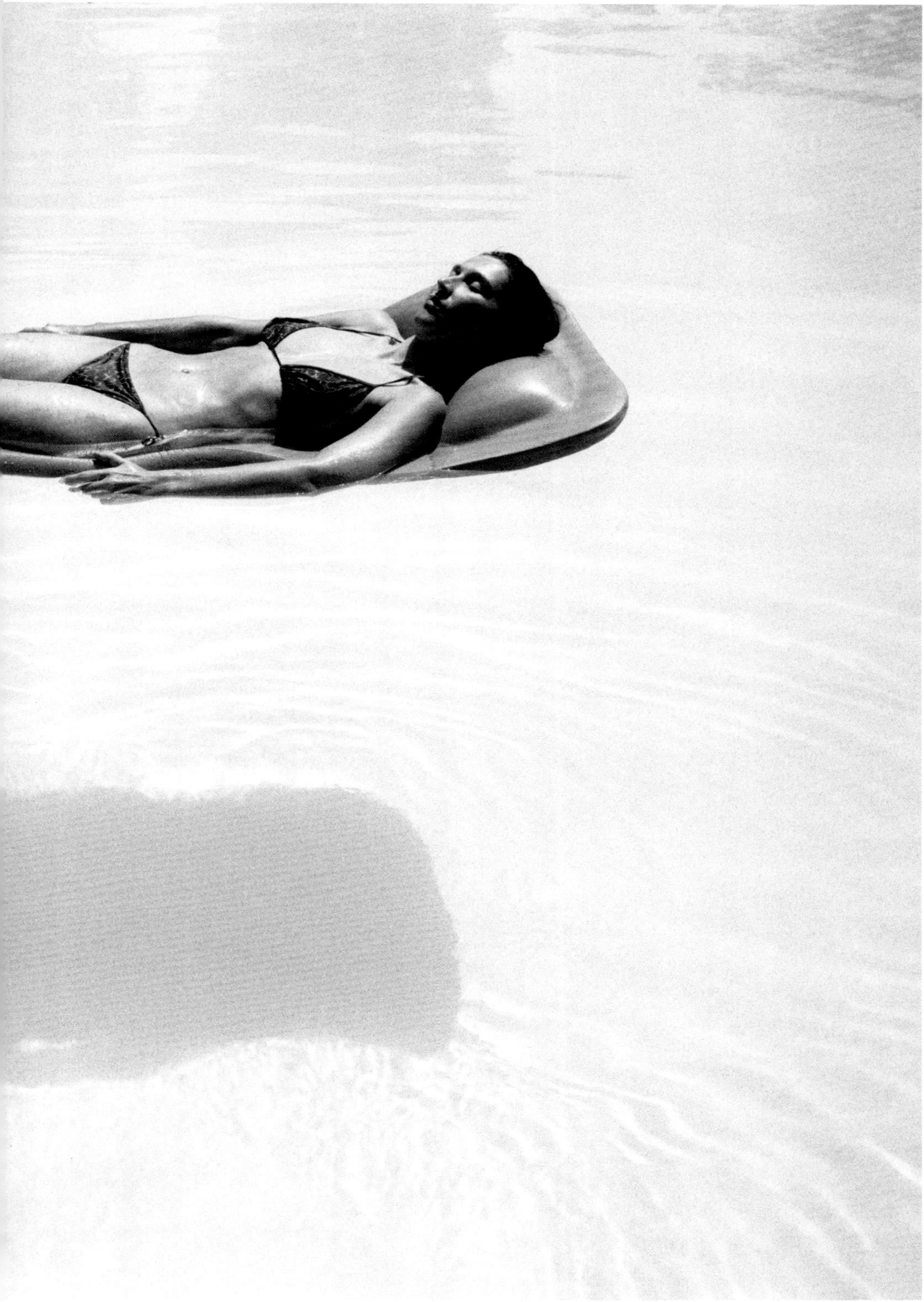

In the spring of 1998, as Moscow was falling into default, I fell in love. The city was in political chaos; dizzy and breathless, I barely noticed. The blow for me came shortly afterwards, when *The New York Times* sent me to live in Rome. On my last morning in Russia, I said goodbye to Sylvie at 5 a.m. and then walked from her home across the Moscow River to my apartment, where twenty-two pieces of luggage—the entirety of my possessions—were waiting to accompany me to Italy.

Rome was sweltering and beautiful, another world in more ways than one. As a friend had said to comfort me, when I'd received the assignment, "Imagine living in a city where you can use the words 'lunch' and 'outside' in the same sentence!" Yet I felt unable to enjoy it alone. I implored Sylvie to visit, both hopeful and apprehensive, not knowing what our love would feel like in another country. A few weeks later, she got on a plane to Rome.

While she was in the air that Friday, an editor in New York called, asking me to fly to Nairobi to cover the aftermath of the bombing of the American Embassy. I refused. I had a hard time believing the words as

Love in a Warm Climate

Umbria
13 August 1998

they came out of my mouth; it was as if I were listening to someone else, because it was the first time I had ever turned down a major assignment. After I put the phone down, I couldn't tell if I felt more guilty or elated.

The heat was scorching that week. Sylvie and I spent several days in Rome, walking countless miles through its cobbled streets, the labyrinth of the city serving as a prism for our emotions. Then we left to stay with some friends in Umbria. Even in the hills of central Italy, the sun was relentless, and the guests took refuge wherever they could.

Late one morning, while searching for Sylvie, I found her alone in the swimming pool, lying on an inflatable mattress. Judging from the shadow in the picture, it must have been around midday; I tiptoed to the water's edge. The shutter of the Leica rangefinder was so quiet that I was able to fire off several frames before Sylvie opened her eyes and saw me standing to the side.

Of all the photographs that have seared themselves on my memory, with and without my wishes, this is the one that makes me happiest. It triggers a sensation of intense warmth in which even the small details of that moment—the songs of the cicadas in the cypresses, the symmetric ripples lapping the pool's edge—are perfectly captured. I can always shut my eyes and conjure up Sylvie floating—or is it flying?—just in front of me.

Three years later, when I was in Afghanistan, Sylvie would be pregnant with our son; in 2003, as I was heading to Baghdad with the U.S. Marines, she was pregnant again, with our daughter. On each of those journeys we held daily satellite phone calls, our conversations filled with the uncertain words of two people inhabiting two contradictory worlds and not knowing when, if ever, they would see each other again. And perhaps there are no words to traverse such vast emotional and physical distances, which is why this photograph has always been so precious to me. Sometimes the camera will find a moment of happiness that initially seems insignificant but with time takes on another meaning. Whenever I looked at this photograph, often in a place of true darkness, I could return for a few priceless moments to Sylvie's side and that perfect day, when there was not a cloud in sight.

All photographs and texts by James Hill

Editor
Alice Truax

Copy Editor
Elizabeth Pearson-Griffiths

Image Processing
Kehrer Design (René Henoch)

Design
Kehrer Design (Hannah Feldmeier)

Production
Kehrer Design (Andreas Schubert)

Printed and bound in Germany

ISBN 978-3-86828-459-1

Kehrer Heidelberg Berlin
www.kehrerverlag.com